BRIAN CLARK

CORNELSEN SENIOR ENGLISH LIBRARY

Whose Life Is It Anyway?

Cornelsen

Brian Clark **Whose Life Is It Anyway?**

Herausgegeben von:
Prof. Dr. Albert-Reiner Glaap

Verlagsredaktion:
Ralph Williams

Umschlaggestaltung:
Cornelsen Verlag Design; *Bildrecherche*: Josephine Wolff

Umschlagfoto:
© Nino Mascardi / Stone / Getty Images

Typografie:
Annika Preyhs für Buchgestaltung+

Technische Umsetzung:
Britta Dieterle, Buch und Gestaltung

www.cornelsen.de

1. Auflage, 1. Druck 2012

Alle Drucke dieser Auflage sind inhaltlich unverändert
und können im Unterricht nebeneinander verwendet werden.

Druck: H. Heenemann, Berlin

ISBN 978-3-06-033031-7

Inhalt gedruckt auf säurefreiem Papier aus nachhaltiger Forstwirtschaft.

CONTENTS

Abbreviations and Annotations

adj	adjective	**fml**	formal
adv	adverb	**infml**	informal
AE	American English	**jdm./jdn.**	jemandem/en
BE	British English	**n**	noun
ca.	circa; about	**sb.**	somebody
cf.	confer; see	**sl**	slang
e.g.	exempli gratia; for example	**sth.**	something
esp.	especially	**usu.**	usually
etc.	et cetera; and so on	**v**	verb

The annotations are arranged chronologically; the first time a word is used is where you will find it explained.

Dear Student,

Plays are written to live in the theatre, so what is this play doing in a classroom?

It's a good question that deserves a little thought. All the arts – painting, sculpture, poetry, dance and so on – have evolved over the history of our species as a means by which we can talk to each other about matters that concern us all. They are a way of bringing us together and making a contribution to solving problems that affect every part of us, our hearts as well as our heads. And theatre is right at the pinnacle of that collective effort.

The playwright can use many of the visual and aural arts to make his play, song, dance, poetry, but the key one is the art of dramatic dialogue, which actually is not like ordinary conversation though he tries very hard to make it seem like that. If you want proof of that, just set a tape recorder on a table in a room while a group is talking and then transcribe what you hear. It will be very different from a play!

So to make our experience in the theatre as full as it can be, it is worth studying dramatic dialogue on its own, finding out how it works, what makes it good – or awful! How has the playwright constructed his characters? How has he told the story? How has he managed to hold our attention for a couple of hours sitting still in a dark room? In seeking to answer those questions, the play will open itself up to you.

I hope it does and I hope you enjoy the process. Most of all I hope you will have a chance to experience the play in its totality – in a theatre. And finally I hope that if you do manage to do that, you will find your experience much more complete, much more enjoyable.

Brian Clark

THE CHARACTERS

CLAIRE HARRISON (35): the patient, a sculptor

SISTER ANDERSON: a ward sister

NURSE KAY SADLER: a student nurse

JOHN: a ward orderly

DR. DAVID SCOTT: a registrar

DR. MICHAEL EMERSON: a consultant physician

MRS. MARGARET BOYLE: a social worker

MISS HELEN HILL: a solicitor

MRS. JUSTICE MILLHOUSE: a judge

A judge's clerk (non-speaking)

ACT ONE

SISTER ANDERSON *(50) and* NURSE KAY SADLER *(18) enter the hospital room of* CLAIRE HARRISON *(35) with a trolley.* CLAIRE *is a tetraplegic, completely still in her bed.*

SISTER Good morning, Claire. A new face for you today.

CLAIRE Hello, new face.

KAY: Hello.

SISTER *operates bed to the flat position.*

CLAIRE: I'm afraid I can't offer you my hand. You'll just have to make do with my backside like all the other nurses.

They lower the bed.

CLAIRE (CONT'D): Going down – Obstetrics, Gynaecology, Lingerie, Rubberware …

They begin to massage her.

CLAIRE (CONT'D): It's funny you know. I used to dream of situations like this. Lying on a bed being massaged … though actually in my fantasy it was by two gorgeous men, incredibly strong, but unbelievably gentle.

SISTER (MOCK SERIOUS): If you go on like this, Claire, I won't be able to send my student nurses in here.

The telephone rings outside in Sister Anderson's office.

SISTER (CONT'D): Can you manage for a moment, Nurse?

KAY: Oh, yes Sister.

1 **(ward) sister**: *Stationsschwester* **nurse**: *Krankenschwester* 2 **trolley**: small table on wheels 11 **obstetrics** [əb'stetrɪks]: *Geburtshilfe* **gynaecology** [ˌgaɪnə'kɒlədʒi]: *Gynäkologie* **lingerie** ['lænʒəri]: women's underwear 12 **rubber wear**: *medizinische Handschuhe* 18 **mock serious**: pretending to be serious 21 **can you manage?**: can you do that without help?

SISTER: Wipe your hands and put these pillows behind Claire … we don't want to have her on the floor.

CLAIRE: On the floor! In my dreams! I remember being once …

SISTER ANDERSON *goes to her office to answer the telephone.*

CLAIRE (CONT'D): What's your name?

KAY: Kay Sadler, but my friends call me Flea.

CLAIRE (HUSHED TONES): Don't let Sister Anderson hear you say that.

KAY: Why not?

CLAIRE: Well, you must answer "Kay" with a smile that is full of warmth, but not too personal.

KAY: I'm sorry.

CLAIRE: I'm not. I'm glad you're called Flea. I'll call you Flea when we're alone, just you and me, having my backside caressed …

KAY: I'm rubbing your heels.

CLAIRE: Don't spoil it. After all, it doesn't matter. I can't feel anything wherever you are. Am I your first backside?

KAY: Yes. I'm still in Primary Training. But I finish next week.

CLAIRE: And you can't wait to get here full-time.

KAY: I'll be glad to finish.

CLAIRE: Students are all the same.

KAY: Were you a teacher?

CLAIRE: Tut, tut. Second lesson: You mustn't use the past tense.

KAY: What do you mean?

1 **wipe**: *abwischen* 6 **flea**: *Floh* 13 **caress**: stoke in a sensual way 15 **rub**: *massieren* 23 **tut tut**: noise you make to show disapproval

CLAIRE: You said "Were you a teacher?" You should have said "Are you a teacher?" I mean, you are now part of the optimism industry. Everyone who deals with me acts as though, for the first time in the history of medical science, a ruptured spinal column will heal itself – it's just a bit of a bore waiting for it to happen.

KAY: I'm sorry.

CLAIRE: Don't be. You're a breath of fresh air.

KAY: What do you mean?

CLAIRE: … I'm surrounded by what is called professionalism. Everyone deals with me through a filter of codes and euphemisms. Don't get me wrong, I don't think they're bad or cruel or anything. But I cannot allow myself to feel that they care for me, personally. They can't. There are too many of us and they have lives to lead themselves. So I have to develop a carapace …

KAY: A what … ?

CLAIRE: A shell, hard. Because I can't get to them, not in any profound way, I can't let them get to me. But you're an innocent – just for a while. And I was enjoying that. A breath of fresh air.

KAY: But don't you have family, a boyfriend ... ?

CLAIRE: I did. I've sent them all away.

KAY: But that's terrible.

CLAIRE: No. I have things to do and I must do them by myself. I must try not to hurt them … and …

SISTER ANDERSON *comes back.*

CLAIRE (CONT'D): Good phone call, Sister?

SISTER: Just routine.

4 **rupture**: *zerren* 5 **bore**: boring thing 10 **euphemism**: indirect word or phrase used to refer to sth. embarrassing 14 **carapace** ['kærəpeɪs]: hard shell

CLAIRE: Only the heavy breathing, you mean? No definite suggestions. What's the good of phone sex if it's only routine?

KAY *laughs.*

SISTER: I'm glad you two are getting along.

CLAIRE: I've been giving her the low-down on nursing from the consumer's point of view, but she still wants to come here.

SISTER: If she still feels like that after being five minutes with you – we'll make a nurse of her yet.

CLAIRE: I'm not sure how to take that … Lying down I suppose.

SISTER ANDERSON *and* KAY *move* CLAIRE'S *bed back into position.* SISTER ANDERSON *operates the bed to a sitting position.*

SISTER: Night Sister said you slept well.

CLAIRE: Ah – then I fooled her … After her last round a boy friend of mine came in and smuggled me out … we went midnight skateboarding.

SISTER: Oh, yes … I hope it was fun …

CLAIRE: It was alright … the only problem was: I was the skateboard.

SISTER ANDERSON *and* KAY *adjust* CLAIRE *in the bed, replace pillows.*

SISTER: There, that's better. Comfortable?

CLAIRE: It's so beautifully made, I can't feel a thing.

SISTER: I'll see you later.

SISTER ANDERSON *and* KAY *cross downstage.*

KAY: Sister … how long has she been here?

SISTER: Five months.

KAY: Will she ever get better?

4 **get along**: *sich gut verstehen* 5 **give sb. the low-down**: tell sb. important information 9 **take sth. lying down**: accept sth. without complaining

SISTER: It's very unlikely.

KAY: What will happen to her?

SISTER: When we have her fully stabilised, she'll be transferred to a long-stay hospital.

KAY: For the rest of her life?

SISTER: Yes.

JOHN, *(20) a West Indian orderly in a white coat over jeans and a T-shirt, comes along the corridor with cleaning materials.*

JOHN: Morning, Sister.

SISTER: Morning, John. Are you going to Claire Harrison's room?

JOHN: That's right.

SISTER: Good. Take the trolley into the ward, nurse, and start on Mr. Phillips.

SISTER ANDERSON *goes to check a file in her office.* JOHN *goes into* CLAIRE'S *room.*

JOHN: Morning.

CLAIRE: Morning, John. How's things?

JOHN: Just fine …

JOHN *dusts around room and empties a wastebasket.*

CLAIRE: By God, you can move, John.

JOHN: Tell that to Sister Anderson, will you? Every time I sit down – that's the very second she comes into the room and sees me doing nothing.

CLAIRE (PLAYFULLY): Well, I think you move beautifully.

JOHN: It's being black.

17 **How's things?**: How are you? 19 **wastebasket**: rubbish bin

CLAIRE: It's being what?

JOHN (CLICKING HIS FINGERS): Black! We can sing, we can dance, we've all got rhythm …

CLAIRE: Hey! I wasn't patronising you. You forget. I was a sculptor. I studied movement.

JOHN: How's that? Statues don't move.

CLAIRE: … They do in a way.

JOHN: Well, if ever Nelson steps off his column, it'll be a helluva lot worse than a pigeon crapping on your head.

He sits down. SISTER ANDERSON *enters.*

SISTER: John …

JOHN *jumps to his feet.*

SISTER (CONT'D): Dr. Scott will probably be early this morning. Dr. Emerson's making rounds today.

She goes back out.

JOHN: You see what I mean? The moment I sit on that stool, the Sister appears. I tell you, my arse is magic!

CLAIRE: You never said a truer word …

JOHN: Watch it, lady!

CLAIRE: Watch it? I can't take my eyes off it!

JOHN (BUSTLING AROUND AGAIN): I'm sorry, I don't have time to be seduced. But maybe after the doctors' rounds.

4 **patronise sb.**: (here) be friendly to sb. because you think they aren't clever **sculptor**: artist who makes statues 8 **Nelson**: Lord Horatio Nelson, whose statue is on the top of a column in the centre of Trafalgar Square, London **a helluva lot**: a hell of a lot (much) 9 **pigeon**: *Taube* **crap** (sl): *defäkieren* 14 **make rounds**: (of a doctor) visit patients for quick check-ups 21 **bustle**: move in a hurried way 22 **seduce**: *verführen*

CLAIRE: The visitation of the gods.

JOHN: Oh, yes – they have a very high opinion of their own opinion.

CLAIRE: What happened to the other guy that used to work here? What was his name? Marcus, that's it. Whatever happened to dear Marcus?

JOHN: They come and they go … I think he left to get married up North somewhere.

CLAIRE: Marcus? Married? Who to? A lorry driver?

JOHN: Bitchy, bitchy.

CLAIRE: No. Envy, envy. From where I'm lying, if I could make it at all, even by myself, it would be heaven.

Pause.

CLAIRE (CONT'D): I'm sorry … I'm feeling sorry for myself today. Can't even say I got out of the wrong side of the bed.

JOHN *laughs.*

CLARE: Anyway, how long will you be staying?

JOHN: Just until we go professional.

CLAIRE: Doing what?

JOHN: Music. I'm in a rap group. And we're getting around a bit … in the clubs.

CLAIRE: What do you play?

JOHN: I program the drum machines.

CLAIRE: Ah … not the real thing anymore … Even music these days depends on machines. I'm sure you could even play me!

JOHN: Why not?

1 **visitation** (fml): visit 10 **envy**: *Neid* 14 **get out of the wrong side of bed**: start the day in a bad mood 24 **depend on sth.**: need sth. in order to work

He puts down his mop and strikes CLAIRE *very lightly up and down her body like a drum kit while "beat-boxing".* CLAIRE *is delighted.*

DR. SCOTT *(29) comes in.* JOHN *stops.*

CLAIRE (TO JOHN): It just isn't your day, is it?

DR. SCOTT: What's going on here?

CLAIRE: He's just testing my reflexes.

DR. SCOTT: Oh … and how are they?

JOHN: Do you want the bad news first?

JOHN *goes towards the door.*

CLARE: Hey John! If Dr Scott could drill some holes in my head, you could blow in my ear and play me like an ocarina.

JOHN (SMILING): I'll see you later.

DR. SCOTT: You're bright and chirpy this morning.

CLAIRE (IRONICALLY): It's marvellous, you know. The courage of the human spirit.

DR. SCOTT (DRYLY): Nice to hear the human spirit's okay. How's the lungs?

He takes his stethoscope from his pocket and puts it to CLAIRE'S *chest.*

CLAIRE (MIMICKING A TIMPANI): Bi-Boom.

DR. SCOTT *reacts to the loud noise in his stethoscope.*

CLAIRE (CONT'D): Sorry.

He continues to listen. CLAIRE *mimes an animated monologue. As* DR. SCOTT *removes the stethoscope:*

1 **strike**: hit 4 **it isn't your day**: It's not a good day for you 11 **ocarina**: small muscial instrument that you blow into 13 **chirpy**: in a good mood 19 **timpani**: set of metal drums 22 **mime**: move your lips to silently imply speech **animated**: energetic

CLAIRE (CONT'D): … which proves that you should never do it in a lift!

DR. SCOTT *looks at her, unimpressed. Pause.*

CLAIRE (CONT'D): So what does it say?

DR. SCOTT: Say?

CLAIRE: My heart. What secrets does it tell?

DR. SCOTT: It was just telling me that it's better off than it was six months ago.

CLAIRE: It's a brave heart. It keeps its secrets well.

DR. SCOTT: And what are they?

CLAIRE: Did you hear it going Bi-Boom, like that? Two beats?

DR SCOTT: Of course.

CLAIRE: Well, I'll tell you. That's because it's broken, broken in two. But each part carries on bravely yearning for a man in a white coat.

DR. SCOTT: And I thought it was the systolic and diastolic heart beats.

CLAIRE: How romantic …

DR. SCOTT *looks at her sharply.*

CLAIRE (CONT'D): So Emerson's making rounds this morning?

DR. SCOTT: That's right.

CLAIRE: I suppose he'll sweep in here like Zeus from Olympus, with his attendant nymphs and swains.

7 **better off**: in a better condition 14 **yearn for sth.**: want sth. very much 16 **systolic**: part of the heart's rythm when it pumps blood **diastolic**: part of the heart's rythm when it fills with blood 22–23 **with his attendant nymphs and swains**: *mit seinem Gefolge hilfreicher Geister*

DR. SCOTT: I don't think that's fair.

CLAIRE: Why not?

DR. SCOTT: He cares – he cares a lot.

CLAIRE: But what about?

DR. SCOTT: His patients.

CLAIRE: Really …

DR. SCOTT: He does. When you first came in, he worked his guts out to keep you going. He cares.

CLAIRE: But soon we'll have to ask the question "why?"

DR. SCOTT: Why?

CLAIRE: Why he bothered. You remember the mountain laboured and brought forth not a man but a mouse. It was a big joke. On the mouse. If you're as insignificant as that, who needs a mountain for a mummy?

DR SCOTT *makes a quick note on the chart.*

DR. SCOTT: I'll see you later … with Dr. Emerson.

CLAIRE: And Cupbearers Limited.

He goes out and meets SISTER ANDERSON *at the door of her office.*

DR. SCOTT: Sister, it's Miss Harrison. She seems a little agitated this morning.

SISTER: Yes. She's beginning to realise what she's up against.

DR. SCOTT: I'm upping her sedation – just a little.

SISTER *makes a note in her office and leaves.*

KAY *enters* CLAIRE'S *room with a feeding cup.*

7–8 **work your guts out** (infml): work very hard **keep sb. going**: (here) keep sb. alive 19 **agitated**: worried 21 **be up against sth.**: have sth. as a problem 22 **sedation**: *Beruhigungsmittel*

CLAIRE: An acolyte, bearing a cup.

KAY: I beg your pardon?

CLAIRE: Nothing. I was joking. It's nothing.

KAY: It's coffee.

CLAIRE: Now you're joking. What you have there is a coffee-flavoured milk drink.

KAY: Don't you like it?

CLAIRE: What I would like is some real coffee – hot, black and bitter so I could chew it.

KAY: I'll ask Sister Anderson.

CLAIRE: I wouldn't bother.

KAY: Why not?

CLAIRE: Because in an hour's time you'll be bringing round a little pill that's designed to insert rose-coloured filters in front of my eyes. It will calm me and soothe me and make me forget for a while that you can walk out of here tonight and make love to your boyfriend.

KAY: I … I'm …

CLAIRE (GENUINELY CONCERNED): I'm sorry. Really, I am sorry. I don't mean to take it out on you – it's not your fault. You're only the vestal virgin … sorry I said virgin.

KAY: I think you'd better drink your coffee before it gets cold.

She feeds CLAIRE *a little, sip by sip.*

1 **acolyte**: person who helps a priest in religious services 9 **chew**: *kauen*
14 **rose-coloured filters**: magic glasses that make you see a perfect version of your surroundings 15 **soothe sb.**: make sb. feel more comfortable 19 **genuinely**: honestly 21 **vestal virgin**: a young woman who served Vesta, the Roman goddess of the house 23 **sip**: drink a very small amount

CLAIRE: You know if you spilled that on the sheet it wouldn't even stain.

KAY: Probably not.

CLAIRE: What made you become a nurse?

KAY: I'm not a nurse yet.

CLAIRE: Oh, yes, you are ...

KAY *smiles.*

KAY: I always wanted to. And what made you become a sculptor?

CLAIRE: Hey! You're learning too fast!

KAY: What do you mean?

CLAIRE: When you get a personal question, just ignore it – change the subject or better still, ask another question back.

KAY *smiles.*

CLAIRE (CONT'D): Didn't your tutor tell you that?

KAY: Something like it.

CLAIRE: It's called being professional, isn't it?

KAY: I suppose so.

CLAIRE: They should put a sign up in here, you know, "Patients are requested not to ask for credit for their intelligence, as refusal often offends."

KAY: You sound angry. I hope I ...

CLAIRE: Not with you, Flea. Not at all. With myself I expect. Don't say it. That's futile, isn't it?

KAY *smiles.*

SISTER ANDERSON *comes in.*

1 **spill**: *verschütten* 23 **futile**: useless

SISTER: Have you finished, Nurse? Dr. Emerson is here.

KAY: Yes Sister. I'm just coming.

SISTER: And straighten this sheet.

She exits.

CLAIRE: Hospitals are weird places. Broken necks are acceptable, but a wrinkled sheet!

KAY *smooths the bed. She goes out as* DR. EMERSON *(41), dressed in an Armani suit and subtly patterned shirt comes in with* SISTER ANDERSON *and* DR. SCOTT.

DR. EMERSON: Morning.

CLAIRE: Good morning.

DR. EMERSON: How are you this morning?

CLAIRE: As you can see, racing around all over the place.

DR. EMERSON: So I hear. Had a lot of complaints. You've knocked down three nurses already. We don't allow running in the corridors.

CLAIRE *chuckles.*

DR. EMERSON *picks up the chart and notes from the bottom of the bed.*

DR. EMERSON (CONT'D) (TO DR. SCOTT): You've increased the Librium, I see.

DR. SCOTT: Yes.

DR. EMERSON: Her renal function looks much improved.

DR. SCOTT: Yes, the blood urea is back to normal and the cultures are sterile.

8 **subtly patterned**: *mit einem feinen Muster* 17 **chuckle**: laugh quietly
20 **Librium**: calming drug 22 **renal**: relating to the kidneys 23 **urea**: substance found in urine **culture**: group of cells

DR. EMERSON: Good … good. We'd better keep an eye on it, just in case.

DR. SCOTT: Yes, of course …

DR. EMERSON: Good … Well Claire, we seem to be out of the wood now …

CLAIRE: So when are you going to discharge me?

DR. EMERSON: You'll certainly be leaving us soon.

CLAIRE: Discharged or transferred?

DR. EMERSON: This unit is for critical patients; when we have reached a position of stability, then you can be looked after in a much more comfortable, quiet hospital.

CLAIRE: Ah, I see. You only grow the vegetables here – the vegetable store is somewhere else.

DR. EMERSON (GRINNING): Well first we're entering you in the local flower show. We think we have a great chance in the class for the wittiest carrot.

CLAIRE *grins.*

CLAIRE: Spell it out for me, please. What chance have I of being only partly dependant on nursing?

DR. EMERSON: It's impossible to say with certainty what the prognosis of any case is. Especially at this time with enormous amounts of research into spinal cord injury, fundamental research into neurons, synapses, astrocytes, microglia. It seems it may be possible to induce regeneration by the use of stem cells. There's …

1 **keep an eye on sth.**: keep checking sth. 4 **out of the wood** (infm): safe
6 **discharge** (v): let go 16 **witty**: clever and funny 22 **spinal cord**: *Rückenmark*
23 **neurons, artrocytes, microglia**: cells in the body 24 **stem cell**: *Stammzelle*

CLAIRE: Strings of name's don't help. I know how much effort is going into research but what time scale are we talking about here? Do you believe I will ever walk again? Or at least in the next … ten to fifteen years?

DR. EMERSON: Not that quickly but …

CLAIRE: Or recover the use of my arms in the same time scale?

DR. EMERSON: No.

CLAIRE: Thank you.

DR. EMERSON: For what?

CLAIRE: Your honesty.

DR. EMERSON: Known for it. All over the world.

CLAIRE: Oh, good, good.

DR. EMERSON: Dr. Scott has prescribed something which will help.

CLAIRE: Good, good.

DR. EMERSON (TO DR. SCOTT): You might also get Mrs. Boyle along …

CLAIRE: Oh, yes, what a good idea. I wish I'd thought of that. Jot that down.

DR. SCOTT (TO DR. EMERSON): Yes, of course.

DR. EMERSON (TO CLAIRE): Listen, you'll be surprised how many things you'll be able to do. Goodbye.

CLAIRE: Good. Goodbye. Thank you for coming. Lovely to chat with you. Do drop in again any time you're passing.

DR. SCOTT, DR. EMERSON *and* SISTER ANDERSON *go into the corridor area.*

1 **strings of sth.**: (here) lists of sth. 6 **recover sth.**: (here) get sth. back
13 **prescribe**: *verschreiben* 15 **get sb. along**: bring sb. 17–18 **jot sth. down**: take a note of sth. 23 **drop in**: visit

DR. EMERSON: Shit! A woman as bright as that ... What dose was it you prescribed?

DR. SCOTT: Five milligrams tds.

DR. EMERSON: We'll see how that goes ... We ought to aim to get her moved in a month at most. These beds are very precious.

DR. SCOTT: Yes.

DR. EMERSON: Thank you, David. I must rush. Committee meeting. A board full of accountants. I'd rather have my prostate examined.

He goes. DR. SCOTT *and* SISTER ANDERSON *walk around to the Nurses' Room.*

DR. SCOTT: Sister, did you get that Ativan for Miss Harrison?

SISTER: Yes, I was going to give her the first at twelve o'clock.

DR. SCOTT: Give her one now, will you ... ?

He begins to walk away, then turns.

DR SCOTT: On second thoughts ... give it to me. I want a word with her.

She hands DR. SCOTT *a small cup with the pill in it.*

DR. SCOTT: Thank you.

He walks to CLAIRE'S *room and goes in.*

DR. SCOTT (CONT'D): Hello, again. I've brought something to help you.

CLAIRE: My God, they've got some highly qualified nurses here.

DR. SCOTT: Nothing but the best in this hospital.

1 **bright**: clever **dose**: *Dosierung* 3 **tds**: to be taken three times a day
11 **Ativan**: drug with calming effects

CLAIRE: You're spoiling me, you know, Doctor. If this goes on I shall demand that my next enema is performed by no less than the Director of Nursing.

DR. SCOTT: Well, it wouldn't be the first she's done, or the thousandth either.

CLAIRE: She worked up through the ranks, did she?

DR. SCOTT: They all do.

DR. SCOTT *attempts to give her the pill.*

CLAIRE: Just now, for one or two glorious minutes, I felt like a human being again.

DR. SCOTT: Good.

He attempts to give her the pill again.

CLAIRE: And now you're going to spoil it.

DR. SCOTT: How?

CLAIRE: With this.

DR. SCOTT: Dr. Emerson and I both agreed you needed this.

CLAIRE: You both watched me – disturbed, worried even, that you can't do anything for me – nothing that really matters. I'm paralysed and you're impotent. This disturbs you. As someone dedicated to an active sympathy you find it hard to accept that you're impotent. The only thing you can do is to stop me thinking about it – that is – stop me disturbing you. So I get the tablet and you get the tranquillity …

DR. SCOTT: That's a tough diagnosis.

CLAIRE: Is it so far from the truth?

1 **spoil**: (here) *verwöhnen* 2 **enema**: *Darmspülung* 9 **glorious**: amazing, beautiful
13 **spoil**: (here) *verderben* 17 **disturb sb.**: make sb. feel uncomfortable
23 **tranquillity**: peace 24 **tough**: difficult to accept

DR. SCOTT: There may be an element of truth in it, but it's not the whole story.

CLAIRE: No, I don't suppose it is.

DR. SCOTT: After all, there is no point in worrying unduly – you know the facts. It's no use banging your head against a wall.

CLAIRE: But if the only feeling I have is in my head and I want to feel, I might choose to bang it against a wall.

DR. SCOTT: And if you damage your head?

CLAIRE: You mean, go crazy?

DR. SCOTT: Yes.

CLAIRE: Then that would be the final catastrophe, but I'm not crazy yet. My consciousness is the only thing I have and I must reserve the right to use it and, as far as possible, act on any conclusions it may come to.

DR. SCOTT: Of course.

CLAIRE: Good. Then if you want tranquillity, you take the pill.

DR. SCOTT *attempts to give her the pill again.*

DR. SCOTT: Come on.

CLAIRE: No, I'm not going to.

DR. SCOTT: It is prescribed.

CLAIRE: Oh, come on, Doctor. I know everyone around here acts as though those little pieces of paper have just been handed down from Sinai. But the writing on those tablets isn't in Hebrew.

DR. SCOTT (PUTTING PILL BACK INTO CUP): Well, you aren't due for it till midday. We'll see …

4 **unduly**: unnecessarily 5 **bang your head against a wall**: suffer for no reason 12 **consciousness**: *Bewusstsein* **reserve**: (here) keep 23 **Sinai**: mountain where Moses received the ten commandments **tablet**: flat stone with writing on it 24 **be due for sth.**: (here) be expected to have sth.

CLAIRE: That's what I always say. If you don't know whether to take a tranquilliser or not – sleep on it. When you tell Dr. Emerson, impress on him that I don't need it.

DR. SCOTT *nods noncommittally.*

CLAIRE (CONT'D): Won't you?

DR. SCOTT *leaves and goes to the Nurses' Office.*

DR. SCOTT: I haven't given it to her … leave it for a while, will you.

SISTER: Did you alter the notes?

DR. SCOTT: No … not yet.

SISTER ANDERSON *picks up a pile of notes and begins writing. Cross Fade on sluice room.*

KAY *enters with trolley. She is taking kidney dishes and instruments out of the steriliser.* JOHN *creeps up behind her and seizes her around the waist.* KAY *jumps, utters a muffled scream and drops an instrument.*

KAY: Don't do that …

JOHN: I couldn't help myself, honest, your honour. There was this vision in white – like an angel. I just had to touch her.

KAY *replaces the forceps and turns to* JOHN.

JOHN (CONT'D): What's a nice girl like you doing in a place like this?

KAY: Sterilising the instruments …

JOHN *gasps and holds his groin.*

JOHN: Don't say things like that! Just the thought …

KAY *returns to her work.*

3 **impress sth. on sb.**: make sth. clear to sb. 4 **noncommittally**: in a way that makes it unclear what you will actually do 8 **alter**: change 11 **sluice room**: room for cleaning hospital equipment 14 **muffled**: hard to hear 16 **your honour**: form of address for a judge in court 21 **groin** [grɔɪn]: *Leiste*

KAY: I don't know what you're doing in a place like this … It's just a big joke to you.

JOHN: Course it is. You can't take this place seriously …

KAY: Why not?

JOHN: Because it's just the ante-room of the morgue.

KAY: That's terrible! They don't all die.

JOHN: Don't they?

KAY: No! Old Mr. Trevellyan is going out tomorrow.

JOHN: He's had three heart attacks! I just hope they give him a return ticket for the ambulance.

KAY: Would you just let them die? People like Claire Harrison?

She breaks away from him with the trolley.

JOHN: How much does it cost to keep her here? Thousands of pounds a week?

KAY: That's not the point.

JOHN: In Africa children die of diarrhoea. It would cost only a few pence to keep them alive. There's something crazy somewhere.

KAY: That's wrong too – but it wouldn't help just letting Claire die.

She breaks away again.

JOHN (CATCHING HER): Why don't we go out tonight?

KAY: I've got some work to do for my finals.

JOHN: That's precisely it. I'm an expert on anatomy. You must let me help. We could go dancing … Then back to my place for an anatomy lesson.

5 **ante-room**: waiting room **morgue**: where dead bodies are kept 12 **break away**: escape 15 **that's not the point**: that's not the thing under discussion
16 **diarrhoea**: *Durchfall* 21 **finals**: final exams

KAY: Let me get on …

JOHN *dances round her as he raps.*

JOHN: Sister Nurse, you know ya tearin' me apart
I'm cut to the quick and sick in the heart
I said this is the plan: let me give you a scan
An' tonight I'm gonna be your Medicine man
So feel the size of the pulse, raise your eyes to the skies
And hey little sister, let your temp'rature rise
Dis-orderly'll take his little nurse to town
'Cos I need a lotta lovin' till the swelling goes down -

He makes a move on her. KAY *escapes just in time. She backs out of the room and into* SISTER, *who is coming to see what's causing the noise.*

KAY: Sorry, Sister.

SISTER: This hospital exists to cure accidents, not to cause them.

KAY: No … Yes … Sister.

SISTER: Are you going to be all day with that steriliser?

KAY: No Sister.

SISTER *turns to* JOHN.

SISTER: Haven't you any work to do John?

JOHN: Sister, my back is bowed down with the weight of all the work resting on it.

SISTER: Then I suggest you shift some.

JOHN: Right.

JOHN *goes.* SISTER *turns back to* KAY.

1 **get on**: continue 4 **cut to the quick**: cut to the bone (also: emotionally hurt)
9 **orderly**: hospital employee with non-medical duties **disorderly**: out of control
11 **make a move on sb.**: approach sb. in a sexual way 20 **bowed down**: bent
22 **shift sth.**: (here) do sth.

SISTER: And your job is to lower the temperature of the patients, not raise the hopes of the orderlies.

KAY: Yes, Sister.

SISTER ANDERSON *goes into her office.* KAY *exits.*

Cross fade on DR. EMERSON'S *office.* DR. EMERSON *is on the phone.*

DR. EMERSON: Look, Jenkins, I've got four cardiac cases in here at the moment. With that unit I could save at least point five of a nurse a day.

DR. SCOTT *knocks on the door and goes in.* DR. EMERSON *waves* DR. SCOTT *to a seat.*

DR. EMERSON (CONT'D) (STILL ON THE PHONE): Do impress on the trust how much money we'd save in the long run … OK … bye.

He puts the phone down and turns to DR. SCOTT.

DR. EMERSON (CONT'D): Bloody administrators. In this job a degree in accounting would be more valuable to me than my fellowship. Still, what can I do for you?

DR. SCOTT: It's Claire Harrison.

DR. EMERSON: What's wrong?

DR. SCOTT: She doesn't want to take the Ativan. She said she preferred to keep her consciousness clear.

DR. EMERSON: Damn …

DR. SCOTT: … I'm not sure she's not right.

DR. EMERSON: … When you prescribed the drug, you thought she needed it.

DR. SCOTT: Yes.

6 **cardiac case**: patients with heart problems 12 **trust**: (here) organisation that manages finance 15 **fellowship**: senior status at university (here: teaching hospital)

DR. EMERSON: It's a very small dose. The minimum that will have any effect at all. It's not even a psychiatric dose.

DR. SCOTT: I know, but she isn't a psychiatric case, is she?

DR. EMERSON: So, how did you persuade her to take it?

DR. SCOTT: … I didn't.

DR. EMERSON: Now, let's get this clear. This morning when you examined her, you came to a careful and responsible decision that your patient needed Ativan.

DR. SCOTT: Yes.

DR. EMERSON: And yet in spite of two qualified opinions, you accept the decision of someone completely unqualified.

DR. SCOTT: She may be unqualified, but she is the one affected.

DR. EMERSON: Ours was an objective, hers a subjective decision.

DR. SCOTT: But isn't this a case where a subjective decision may be more valid? After all, you're both working on the same subject – her body. Only she knows more about how she feels.

DR. EMERSON: But she doesn't know about drugs and their effects.

DR. SCOTT: She can feel their effects directly.

DR. EMERSON: Makes no difference. Her knowledge isn't based on experience of a hundred such cases. She can't know enough to challenge our clinical decisions.

DR. SCOTT: That's what she's doing and she's protesting about the dulling of her consciousness.

DR. EMERSON *walks over to the window to think.* SCOTT *is very uneasy with the confrontation.*

DR. EMERSON: … You think I don't care ?

10 **in spite of sth.**: despite sth. 15 **valid**: reasonable 23 **dull sth.**: make sth. slower and unclear 24 **uneasy**: uncomfortable

DR. SCOTT: No! I think you do.

DR. EMERSON: You're bloody right I care! And so do you. Good! It's why I took you on as my registrar. I'm not interested in doctors who regard their patients as a collection of perambulating symptoms – or in her case supine symptoms, but caring involves professional duty. We can't become bleeding hearts. And the only way we can help Claire Harrison now is help her to maximise whatever powers she retains.

DR. SCOTT: And how does a depressant drug maximise her consciousness?

DR. EMERSON: It will help her to use her consciousness. Look, David, we must help her now to turn her mind to the real problem she has. We must help her to an acceptance of her condition. Only then will her full consciousness be of any use to her at all … You say she refused to take the tablet?

DR. SCOTT *nods.* DR. EMERSON *picks up the telephone and dials. The phone rings in* SISTER ANDERSON'S *office and she picks it up.*

SISTER: Sister Anderson …

DR. EMERSON: This is Dr. Emerson. Could you prepare a syringe with two milligrams of Librium for Claire Harrison?

SISTER: Yes, Doctor.

DR. EMERSON: I'll be down myself immediately to give it to her.

SISTER: Yes, Doctor.

She replaces the telephone and immediately prepares the syringe.

DR. SCOTT: Do you want me to come?

DR. EMERSON: … It won't be necessary.

3 **registrar**: qualified doctor 4 **perambulate**: walk 5 **supine**: lying down
6 **bleeding heart**: person who shows too much sympathy in an annoying way
8 **retain**: (here) still have 19 **syringe**: *Spritze*

DR. SCOTT: Thank you …

DR. EMERSON *moves to the door.*

DR. EMERSON: Claire Harrison is an intelligent, sensitive and articulate woman.

DR. SCOTT: Yes.

DR. EMERSON: But don't undervalue yourself, David. Your first decision was the right one.

He exits and walks around to SISTER ANDERSON'S *office.* DR. SCOTT *sits for a moment, then exits.*

DR. EMERSON (CONT'D): Have you the Librium ready, Sister?

SISTER: Here it is.

DR. EMERSON: Thank you.

She hands him the kidney dish and he takes it. She starts to follow him.

DR. EMERSON (CONT'D): It's all right, Sister. You've plenty of work, I expect.

SISTER: There's always plenty of that.

DR. EMERSON *goes into* CLAIRE'S *room.* SISTER ANDERSON *goes into her office.*

CLAIRE *is asleep. Her radio is on Radio Three.* DR. EMERSON *looks at her and then turns the radio off.* CLAIRE *does not stir. He gently uncovers her arm and quickly ties a tourniquet around her upper arm, He pauses a moment to think then decides and gives an intravenous injection in the vein at the inside of the elbow.*

As he finishes, CLAIRE *opens her eyes and is surprised to see him.*

4 **articulate** (adj): able to express ideas, thoughts and arguments effectively
20 **stir**: move while asleep 21 **tourniquet**: cloth tied tightly around an arm or leg
22 **intravenous injection**: *Spritze*

CLAIRE: Dr. Emerson, I am afraid I must insist that you do not stick that needle in my arm.

DR. EMERSON: It's done now and it was important …

CLAIRE: Who for?

DR. EMERSON: You.

CLAIRE: I'm the best judge of that.

DR. EMERSON: I think not.

CLAIRE: I take it that the injection is one of a series of measures to keep me alive.

DR. EMERSON: You could say that.

CLAIRE: Then it's not important. I've decided that I don't want to stay alive.

DR. EMERSON: But you can't decide that.

CLAIRE: Why not?

DR. EMERSON: You're very depressed.

CLAIRE: Does that surprise you?

DR. EMERSON: No, of course not; it's perfectly natural. Your body has received massive injuries. It takes time to come to an acceptance of the new situation.

CLAIRE: Let me make myself quite clear. I am refusing you permission to give me any kind of sedation or tranquilliser.

DR. EMERSON (LOWERING BED): Please, Claire, rely on us. Of course you're depressed. It's perfectly understandable. It's a stage you're going to have to go through.

CLAIRE: What the hell do I have to do to get someone to listen to me in this place?

DR. EMERSON: Try to get some sleep, and in the morning I'll send someone along to have a chat with you.

He exits.

CLAIRE: What the hell do I have to do?

The lights fade to a night time state. DR. SCOTT *comes down the corridor, pauses for a moment outside* CLAIRE'S *room, looking in at her.* SISTER ANDERSON *crosses below the corridor.*

SISTER: Good night, Doctor.

DR. SCOTT: Good night.

SISTER ANDERSON *exits, then* DR. SCOTT *exits.*

The lights come up. SISTER ANDERSON *and* KAY *come in with a trolley. During the scene they are making* CLAIRE'S *bed.*

SISTER: Good morning, Claire.

CLAIRE: Good morning, Sister.

SISTER: How are you this morning?

CLAIRE: Marvellous.

SISTER (RAISING BED TO SITTING POSITION): The Night Sister said you slept well.

CLAIRE: I had some help, remember.

SISTER: Your eyes are bright this morning.

CLAIRE: I've been thinking.

SISTER: You do too much of that.

CLAIRE: What other activity do you suggest? Jogging maybe? I tell you what, just leave me alone with John for an hour or two and we'll see what he can do for me.

16 **marvellous**: great

SISTER: I'm a Sister, not a madame.

CLAIRE: Sister! You dark horse, you! All this time you've been kidding me. I've been wondering for months how on earth a woman could become a state registered nurse and a Sister and still think you find babies under gooseberry bushes. You've known all along, haven't you?

SISTER: Of course I've known. When I qualified as a midwife I learned that when they find the babies under the gooseberry bushes, they wrap them up in women to keep them warm. I know because it was our job to unwrap them again.

CLAIRE: Anyway, Sister. As I said, I've been thinking, if I'm going to be around for some time, money will help.

SISTER: It usually does.

CLAIRE: Do you remember that solicitor representing my insurance company a few months ago? A Miss Hill, I think. She said she'd come back when I felt better. Do you think you could get her back as soon as possible? I'd feel more secure if we could get the insurance claim settled.

SISTER: Sounds like a good idea.

CLAIRE: You'll ring her?

SISTER: Yes, of course I will. Now back with the spread … back with the sheet … and fold. Are you comfortable now?

CLAIRE *surveys bed.*

CLAIRE: There's a bit of a wrinkle down at the end. It's driving me crazy.

SISTER ANDERSON *smooths the corner on her side.*

1 **madame**: (here) manager of a brothel 2 **dark horse** (infml): person with secrets 5 **gooseberry bush**: *Stachelbeerebusch* 14 **solicitor**: lawyer **insurance**: *Versicherung* 18 **insurance claim**: *Versicherungsanspruch* **settle sth.**: deal with sth. 21 **spread**: (here) bedsheets 24 **wrinkle**: *Falte* 26 **smooth** (v): *glätten*

CLAIRE (CONT'D): Oh, thank you. That's much better. Thank you so much.

SISTER: Now, do you have Miss Hill's number?

CLAIRE: She left a card, it's in my drawer. I'm sorry I haven't had time to tidy them up, I'm run off my feet in this place.

SISTER ANDERSON *goes to the drawer.*

CLAIRE (CONT'D) (TO KAY): Are you qualified to scratch noses?

KAY: Of course.

CLAIRE: You want to give this one a go?

KAY *begins to scratch the left side of* CLAIRE'S *nose.*

CLAIRE (CONT'D): No … other side … That's it … well, a little lower … well, higher … well, just chase it … Thank you.

SISTER: Here it is. Helen Hill, Solicitor. I'll call her.

CLAIRE: Thank you.

SISTER: Now, Claire, there's a Mrs. Boyle to see you.

CLAIRE: Mrs. Boyle? Who's that?

SISTER: A very nice woman.

CLAIRE: Oh, God, must I?

SISTER: Dr. Emerson asked her to stop by.

CLAIRE: Then I'd better see her. If I refuse, he'll probably dissolve her in water and inject her into me.

SISTER ANDERSON *has to choke back a giggle. She then goes out with* KAY.

MARGARET BOYLE *enters. She is about thirty-five, attractive and very professional in her manner. She is a medical social worker.*

5 **be run off your feet**: have too much to do 7 **scratch**: *kratzen* 9 **give sth. a go** (infml): try sth. 19 **stop by**: visit 20 **dissolve**: *auflösen*

MARGARET BOYLE: Claire Harrison?

CLAIRE (CHEERFULLY): I used to be.

MARGARET BOYLE: My name is Margaret Boyle.

CLAIRE: And you've come to cheer me up.

MARGARET BOYLE: I wouldn't put it like that.

CLAIRE: How would you put it?

MARGARET BOYLE: I've come to see if I can help.

CLAIRE: Good. You can.

MARGARET BOYLE: How?

CLAIRE: Go and convince Dr. Frankenstein that he has successfully made his monster and he can now let it go.

MARGARET BOYLE: Dr. Emerson is a first-rate physician. My goodness, they've improved this room.

CLAIRE: Have they?

MARGARET BOYLE: It used to be really dismal. All hospital green and beige. It's surprising what pastel colours will do, isn't it.

CLAIRE: Isn't it? Isn't it just astonishing what pastel colours will do?

MARGARET BOYLE: Really cheerful!

CLAIRE: Yes, it's a remarkably cheerful little room. I so love it. Maybe they should try painting me. I'd hate to be the one thing that ruins the decor.

MARGARET BOYLE: What on earth makes you say that? You don't ruin anything.

4 **cheer sb. up**: make sb. happy 5 **put sth. like that**: say sth. in that way 12 **physician** [fɪ'zɪʃn]: doctor 12–13 **my goodness** (infml): wow 15 **dismal**: depressing 17 **astonishing**: amazing 19 **remarkably**: very

CLAIRE: I know. That was a little … whining. Well, don't let me stop you.

MARGARET BOYLE: Doing what?

CLAIRE: What you came for, I suppose. What do you do? Funny stories? Conjuring tricks? A belly dance? If I have a choice, I'd prefer the conjuring. How about levitation?

MARGARET BOYLE: I'm afraid I've left my magic wand at home.

CLAIRE: Pity.

MARGARET BOYLE: Dr. Emerson tells me that you don't want any more treatment.

CLAIRE: Good.

MARGARET BOYLE: Why good?

CLAIRE: I didn't think he'd heard me.

MARGARET BOYLE: Why not?

CLAIRE: He didn't take any notice.

MARGARET BOYLE: Well, as you can see, he did.

CLAIRE: He sent you … perfect.

MARGARET BOYLE: Why don't you want any more treatment?

CLAIRE: Because I would rather not go on living like this.

MARGARET BOYLE: Why not?

CLAIRE: Isn't it obvious?

MARGARET BOYLE: Not to me. I've seen many patients like you.

CLAIRE: And they all want to live?

1 **whine**: *lamentieren* 5 **conjuring trick**: magical display in which objects appear from nowhere 6 **levitation**: magical display in which objects float in the air
7 **magic wand**: *Zauberstab*

MARGARET BOYLE: Usually.

CLAIRE: Why?

MARGARET BOYLE: They find a new way of life.

CLAIRE: How?

MARGARET BOYLE: Claire, you're going to be surprised at all the things you will be able to do with training and a little patience.

CLAIRE: Such as?

MARGARET BOYLE: We can't be sure yet. But cybernetics, robotics, computer technology, have transformed so many lives. Look at Stephen Hawking. He's …

CLAIRE: Magnificent. As was Christopher Reeve fighting for research into a cure … I really admired that … I salute their choices. I'm not looking for anyone to salute mine, just to recognise my right to make it.

MARGARET BOYLE: … What did you do before the accident?

CLAIRE: I taught in an art school. I was a sculptor.

MARGARET BOYLE: I see.

CLAIRE: That's a tricky one, isn't it? Well, let's think. I know. How about an electronically operated hammer and chisel? Or a cybernetic lump of clay?

She laughs. MARGARET BOYLE *does not join in.*

MARGARET BOYLE: I wouldn't laugh if I were you.

CLAIRE: No, I think you probably wouldn't.

8 **cybernetics**: use of technology to make copies of natural things (i.e. body parts)
10 **Stephen Hawking**: legendary English scientist with motor neurone disease
11 **Christopher Reeve**: former Superman actor who became paralysed from the neck down 12 **salute sth.**: (here) show respect for sth. 18 **tricky**: complicated
2 **chisel**: *Stechbeitel* 20 **lump of sth.**: irregular piece of sth. **clay**: *Ton*

MARGARET BOYLE (REFERRING TO NOTES): I see you have been assessed for occupational therapy. You could certainly control a computer, use voice recognition software, be able to manage computer art. Of course we are not equipped here to make the most of your capabilities, but at Downlands where you will probably go, the OT department is first class.

CLAIRE: I'm sure it is. But it's not good enough, you see. I really have no desire at all to be the object of scientific virtuosity. I have thought things over very carefully. I do have plenty of time for thinking and I have decided that I would rather not go on living with so much effort for so little result.

MARGARET BOYLE: But you can have no idea about what results you can achieve. Of course you are depressed at the moment. And your treatment is designed to help with that.

CLAIRE: But I don't want any more treatment.

MARGARET BOYLE: We can't just stop, just like that.

CLAIRE: Why not?

MARGARET BOYLE: It's the job of the hospital to save life, not to lose it.

CLAIRE: The hospital's done all it can and it wasn't enough.

MARGARET BOYLE: We have to make the best of the situation.

CLAIRE: No. "We" don't have to do anything. I have to do what is to be done and that is to throw in the towel.

MARGARET BOYLE: It's not unusual, you know, for people injured as you are to suffer with this depression for a considerable time before they begin to see that a life is possible.

CLAIRE (CUTTING HER OFF): How long?

MARGARET BOYLE: It varies.

2 **assess**: examine 3 **voice recognition**: *Spracherkennung* 8 **virtuosity**: high level of skill 23 **throw in the towel** (infml): give up 25 **considerable**: large

CLAIRE: Don't hedge.

MARGARET BOYLE: It could be a year or so.

CLAIRE: And it could be for the rest of my life.

MARGARET BOYLE: That would be most unlikely.

CLAIRE: I can't settle for that.

MARGARET BOYLE: I'll see what I can do to get you started on some occupational therapy. We could make a start on the reading system.

CLAIRE: It's marvellous, you know.

MARGARET BOYLE: What is?

CLAIRE: All you people have the same technique. When I say something really awkward you pretend I haven't said anything at all. You're all the bloody same … well, come on, there's another outburst, that should be your cue to comment on the lampshade or the colour of the walls.

MARGARET BOYLE: I'm sorry if I have upset you.

CLAIRE: Of course you've upset me. You and the doctors with your appalling so-called professionalism, which is nothing but a series of verbal tricks to prevent you from relating to your patients as human beings.

MARGARET BOYLE: You must understand; we do have to remain relatively detached in order to help …

CLAIRE: That's fine with me. You just go ahead and detach yourself. Tear yourself off on the dotted line that divides the woman from the social worker and post yourself off to another patient.

1 **hedge** (v): avoid giving a direct answer to a question 5 **settle for sth.**: (here) be satisfied with sth. 12 **awkward**: embarrassing and hard to talk about 14 **outburst**: display of anger **cue**: signal 18 **appalling**: horrible 22 **detached**: *unparteiisch, distanziert* 24 **tear**: *abreißen* **dotted line**: *Punktlinie*

MARGARET BOYLE: You're very upset …

CLAIRE: Christ Almighty, you're doing it again. Listen to yourself. I say something offensive about you and you turn your professional cheek. If you were human, if you were treating me as a human being, you'd tell me to fuck off. Can't you see that this is why I don't want to go on living? I am not human and I'm even more convinced of that by your visit than I was before … So how does that grab you? The very exercise of your so-called professionalism makes me want to die.

She becomes extremely breathless.

MARGARET BOYLE: I'm … Please …

CLAIRE: Go … for God's sake, get out … go on … get out!

MARGARET BOYLE *leaves* CLAIRE'S *room and crosses the stage.*

MARGARET BOYLE: Sister?

CLAIRE: I can't …

MARGARET BOYLE: Sister?

CLAIRE: … breathe.

MARGARET BOYLE *exits.*

MARGARET BOYLE: Sister!

SISTER: What's the matter, Mrs. Boyle?

MRS. BOYLE: It's Miss Harrison … She seems very upset.

CLAIRE: I am … upset!

SISTER ANDERSON *enters.* MRS. BOYLE *follows her.*

SISTER: I would leave her for now, Margaret. We'll send for you when she's better.

2 **Christ Almighty** (sl): curse 3–4 **turn your cheek**: *die andere Wange hinhalten* 7–8 **how does that grab you?**: how does that appear to you? 24 **send for sb.**: ask sb. to come

SISTER ANDERSON *hurries in to* CLAIRE. CLAIRE *is very distressed, rocking her head from side to side desperately short of breath.*

CLAIRE: Sis … ter …

SISTER ANDERSON *reaches for the oxygen mask.*

SISTER: Now, now, Claire. Calm down.

She applies the mask and turns on the oxygen. CLAIRE *gradually becomes calmer.*

SISTER (CONT'D): So why do you go on getting yourself so upset … there's no point.

CLAIRE (MUFFLED): But …

SISTER: Stop talking, Claire. Just relax.

CLAIRE *becomes more calm.* SISTER *sees* KAY *going past.* MARGARET BOYLE *is still hovering.*

SISTER (CONT'D): Nurse, take over here, will you?

KAY (TAKING THE MASK): Hush … Hush …

She holds the mask. CLAIRE *calms down.* SISTER ANDERSON *goes to the door.*

MARGARET BOYLE: Is she all right?

SISTER: Yes perfectly.

MARGARET BOYLE: I'm sorry …

SISTER: No, don't worry. It wasn't your fault. We'll send for you again when she's better.

MARGARET BOYLE: Right … Thank you.

She goes. SISTER ANDERSON *stands at the open door.*

SISTER: Just give her another ten seconds, Nurse.

1 **distressed**: very upset and worried 13 **hover**: (here) wait nearby

KAY: Yes, Sister.

SISTER ANDERSON *takes a pace back behind the door and listens. After ten seconds KAY removes the mask.*

CLAIRE: Oh, she's a shrewd cookie, our Sister.

SISTER ANDERSON *smiles at this.* KAY *glances backward, motions to the door.* CLAIRE *catches on to the reason.*

CLAIRE (CONT'D): It's all right, Sister, you can go now. I'm still alive, damn it.

SISTER ANDERSON *exits, smiling.*

KAY (CHECKING THE DOOR): She's gone.

CLAIRE: I don't want to give her too much satisfaction. Come on, Flea, over here. Cool my fevered brow or something. Come on, be a nurse …

KAY: What upset you?

CLAIRE: Being patronised, I suppose.

KAY: What did you mean about Sister Anderson?

CLAIRE: She knew if she stayed here, I'd shout at her. And that would be bad for me. But if it were you, I wouldn't shout.

KAY: Why?

CLAIRE: A good question. I suppose because you're young and gentle and innocent and she knows that I am not the sort who would shout at you …

KAY: You mean, you would rather patronise me?

CLAIRE (SMILING): … So, you've grown up, become a proper nurse. Well done … But I'm still going to call you Flea!

Kay smiles. Pause.

2 **pace**: step 4 **shrewd cookie** (infml): clever person 5 **motion to sth.**: gesture at sth. 12 **brow**: *Stirn* 21 **gentle**: *sanft* **sort**: (here) kind of person

SISTER ANDERSON *and* DR. SCOTT *come in.*

DR. SCOTT: All right, Nurse.

KAY *leaves.*

CLAIRE: What is this? Piccadilly Circus?

SISTER: Dr. Scott was just passing. Are you feeling better Claire?

CLAIRE: Lovely, thank you, Sister.

SISTER: I made your phone call to Miss Hill. She said she'd try to get in tomorrow.

CLAIRE: Thank you …

SISTER ANDERSON *leaves.*

DR. SCOTT: What was all the fuss about?

CLAIRE: I'm sorry about that. The last thing I want is to bring Dr. Emerson down again with his pharmaceutical truncheon.

DR. SCOTT: I'm … sorry about that.

CLAIRE: I don't suppose it was your fault.

DR. SCOTT: Can I give you some advice?

CLAIRE: Please do.

DR. SCOTT: Take the tablets; the dose is very small – the minimum. They won't really dull your consciousness, not like the injection.

CLAIRE: You're on.

DR. SCOTT: Good … I was glad to hear about your decision to try and settle your insurance claim.

CLAIRE: How did you … ? Oh, I suppose Sister checked with you.

DR. SCOTT: She did mention it …

4 **Piccadilly Circus**: very busy area in London 11 **fuss**: *Getue* 13 **truncheon**: stick that police officers carry as a weapon 20 **You're on** (infml): I accept

DR. SCOTT *begins routinely to use his stethoscope on* CLAIRE'S *chest.*

CLAIRE: Do you like my breasts?

DR. SCOTT: I beg your pardon?

CLAIRE: Do you like my breasts?

Pause.

DR. SCOTT (EMBARRASSED): What an odd thing to say.

CLAIRE: Why? I know you are a doctor but are you telling me you regard them only as mammary glands?

DR. SCOTT: Well, I …

CLAIRE: You never noticed?

DR. SCOTT: Your anatomy is very … You are a beautiful woman.

CLAIRE: You're not so bad yourself. You're perfectly safe, you know.

DR. SCOTT: Of course.

CLAIRE: You do understand then, that I'm not going to leap out of bed and ravish you or anything.

DR. SCOTT: I know.

CLAIRE: Did it embarrass you?

DR. SCOTT: Surprised me.

CLAIRE: And embarrassed you.

DR. SCOTT: Yes, I suppose so.

CLAIRE: But why exactly? I admit that it's unusual for a woman to fish for a compliment on her breasts when only one of them is in bed … One of the people, I mean, not one of the breasts. But that wasn't the reason, was it?

6 **odd**: strange 8 **mammary glands** (fml): anatomical term for breasts
14 **leap**: jump 15 **ravish sb.**: force sb. to have sex 22 **fish for a compliment**: *nach Komplimenten haschen*

DR. SCOTT: I don't think it helps you to talk like this.

CLAIRE: Because I can't do anything about it, you mean.

DR. SCOTT: I didn't mean that exactly.

CLAIRE: I watch you walking around this room, bending over me, examining my body. It's amazing how relaxed a man can be when he is not in the presence of a woman.

DR. SCOTT: I'm sorry if I provoked you … I can assure you …

CLAIRE: You haven't "provoked" me, as you put it, but you are a man and even though I've no feeling in my body I still have a woman's mind. But now, I'm afraid, not a very nice woman. I engage in sexual banter with young orderlies, searching for the double entendre in the most innocent remark. Like a sexually desperate crone. Then they leave the room and I go cold with embarrassment. It's fascinating, isn't it? Laughable. I still have tremendous sexual desire. Do you find that disgusting?

DR. SCOTT: No.

CLAIRE: Pathetic?

DR. SCOTT: Sad.

CLAIRE *starts to break down, then pulls herself together.*

CLAIRE: I'm serious, you know … about deciding to die.

DR. SCOTT: You will get over that feeling.

CLAIRE: How do you know?

DR. SCOTT: From experience.

CLAIRE: That doesn't alter the validity of my decision now.

7 **provoke**: *provozieren* 11 **banter**: joking 12 **double entendre** [ˌdu:bl ɒ̃'tɒ̃drə]: *Doppeldeutigkeit* 13 **crone**: ugly old woman 15 **tremendous**: very big 17 **pathetic**: *erbärmlich* 24 **validity**: state of being logical and true

DR. SCOTT: But if we acted on your decision now, there would be no opportunity for you to change your mind.

CLAIRE: I grant you, I may become lethargic and quiescent. Happy when a nurse comes to put in a new catheter, turn me over or give me an enema. These could become the high points of my day. I might even learn to do wonderful things, like turning the pages of a book or operating a computer with my eyelashes. And you would look at me and say, "Wasn't it worth waiting for?" and I'd say, "Yes," and be proud of my achievements. Really proud. I grant you all that, but it doesn't alter the validity of my present position.

DR. SCOTT: But if you became happy?

CLAIRE: But I don't choose to become happy by becoming the computer section of a complex machine. And morally, you have to accept my decision.

DR. SCOTT: Not according to my morals.

CLAIRE: And why are yours better than mine? I'll tell you why ... They're better because you're more powerful. I am in your power. Well, to hell with a morality that is based on the proposition that might is right.

DR. SCOTT: I must go now. I was halfway through Mr. Patel.

CLAIRE: Oh, really? I thought you were just passing.

DR. SCOTT *walks to the door.*

CLAIRE (CONT'D): Oh, one more thing ...

DR. SCOTT: Yes?

CLAIRE: ... Do you like my breasts?

3 **grant sb. sth.**: admit to sb. that sth. is true **lethargic** [lə'θɑːdʒɪk]: without energy **quiescent** [kwi'esnt]: inactive 19 **to hell with sth.**: expression used to show you don't care about sth. 20 **might**: power

DR. SCOTT (SMILING): … Yes.

CLAIRE: There! That wasn't so hard, was it?

DR. SCOTT *goes to the* SISTER'S *office. He is very upset.* SISTER ANDERSON *passes, sees him and goes in.*

SISTER: Are you all right?

DR. SCOTT: Yes, fine.

SISTER: … Would you like a cup of tea?

DR. SCOTT: Yes, thank you, I would.

KAY *passes with a load of pillows and blankets.*

SISTER: Nurse! Bring a cup of tea for Dr. Scott, please.

KAY: Yes, Sister.

DR. SCOTT: I've never met anyone like Claire Harrison before.

SISTER: No.

DR. SCOTT: She's so … bright … intelligent … she says she wants to die.

SISTER: Lots of patients say that.

DR. SCOTT: I know that, but she means it. It's just a calm, rational decision.

SISTER: I thought this morning, when she was talking about the insurance, she was beginning to plan for the future.

DR. SCOTT: No, not really. That was just to keep us happy. She probably thinks that if she pretends to be planning for the future we'll stop tranquillising her or something like that.

KAY *brings the tea and puts it on the table in front of* DR. SCOTT.

SISTER: Thank you, Nurse.

23 **tranquillise sb.**: use drugs to make sb. calmer

KAY notices that DR. SCOTT *is upset, tense.* SISTER *gives her a look and she exits.*

SISTER (CONT'D): I'm always warning my nurses about getting involved.

DR. SCOTT: And you never do, do you?

SISTER: Never.

DR. SCOTT: You're a liar.

SISTER (MOCK INDIGNATION): Dr. Scott!

DR. SCOTT: It's marvellous, you know. We bring her back to life using everything we've got. We give her back her consciousness, then she says "but how do I use it?" So what do we do? We put her back to sleep.

Lights fade on SISTER'S *office and come up on* CLAIRE'S *room.*

JOHN *goes into* CLAIRE'S *room to empty rubbish and repeats a couple of drum beats on* CLAIRE'S *sleeping body.*

JOHN: Tch, tch.

He shakes his head and exits.

END OF ACT ONE

1 **tense**: *gespannt* **give sb. a look**: look at sb. (often in an angry way)

ACT TWO

SISTER ANDERSON *and* MISS HELEN HILL *(38), formally dressed, enter* CLAIRE'S *room.*

SISTER: A visitor for you Claire – Miss Hill.

MISS HILL: Good afternoon, Miss Harrison.

CLAIRE: Good afternoon. How are you?

MISS HILL: Oh, so, so … You're looking a lot better.

SISTER *has placed a chair by the bed.*

CLAIRE: It's the nursing, you know.

SISTER: I'm so glad you realise it, Claire.

CLAIRE: Oh, I do, Sister. I do.

SISTER ANDERSON, *reluctant to leave, begins to fuss with the bedspread and sheet.*

CLAIRE (CONT'D) (TO MISS HILL): This will only take twenty minutes or so. She's very good at it. Won't do floors or windows of course.

SISTER: Comfortable Claire?

CLAIRE: It's beautifully done.
(TO MISS HILL) Actually, her day job is gift wrapping at Harrods.

SISTER: I'll leave you ladies now.

MISS HILL: Thank you.

SISTER ANDERSON exits to her office.

MISS HILL (CONT'D): You really do look better.

11 **be reluctant to do sth**: *etw. widerstrebend tun* **fuss with sth.**: *viel Aufhebens um etw. machen* 17 **gift wrap** (v): wrap a present with paper **Harrods**: luxury department store in London

CLAIRE: Yes, I'm as well now as I'll ever be …

MISS HILL (UNZIPPING HER BRIEFCASE): I've brought all the papers … things are moving along very satisfactorily now and …

CLAIRE: I don't want to talk about the accident.

MISS HILL: I understand it must be very distressing. I need just a little …

CLAIRE: No, no. It's not that. I don't want to see you about the insurance claim.

MISS HILL: Oh … Sister Anderson said on the phone …

CLAIRE: Yes, I know. Could you come closer?

MISS HILL *moves her chair closer to the bed.*

CLAIRE (CONT'D): No, I mean to the other side.

MISS HILL *crosses to the other side of the bed, away from the door.*

CLAIRE (CONT'D): Look, you do work for yourself? I mean, you don't work for the insurance company?

MISS HILL: No. I'm in a private practice.

CLAIRE: Then there's no reason why you couldn't represent me generally … not just for the insurance claim …

MISS HILL: No. If there's anything I can do …

CLAIRE: There is.

MISS HILL: Yes?

CLAIRE: … Get me out of here.

MISS HILL: … I'm sorry, I don't understand.

CLAIRE: It's quite simple … I can't exist outside the hospital so they've got to keep me here if they want to keep me alive and

2 **unzip sth**: *den Reißverschluss von etw. aufmachen* 16 **private practice**: *Privatpraxis*

they seem intent on doing that. I've decided I don't want to stay in hospital any longer.

MISS HILL: I'm sure the hospital wouldn't keep you here longer than necessary.

CLAIRE: I'm almost completely paralysed and I always will be. I shall never be discharged by any hospital. I've coolly and calmly thought it out and have decided that I would rather not go on. I therefore want to be discharged. To die.

MISS HILL: And you want me to represent you?

CLAIRE: Yes. Tough.

MISS HILL: And what is the hospital's attitude?

CLAIRE: They don't know about it yet. Even tougher.

MISS HILL: This is an enormous step ...

CLAIRE: Miss Hill, with all respect, I know that our hospitals are wonderful. I know that many people have succeeded in making good lives with appalling disabilities. I'm happy for them and respect and admire them. But each person must make their own decision. And mine is to die quietly, with as much dignity as I can muster. And I need your help.

MISS HILL: You do realise what you're asking me to do?

CLAIRE: Yes. I'm not asking you to make any decision about my life and death, just to represent me and my views to the hospital.

MISS HILL: ... Yes, well ... the first thing is to see the doctor in charge.

CLAIRE: That would be Dr. Emerson.

MISS HILL: I'll try and see him now and see where we go from there.

1 **intent on doing sth.**: determined to do sth. 6 **coolly**: without much emotion 18 **dignity**: *Menschenwürde* 19 **muster**: gather, collect 23–24 **in charge**: with the highest level of responsibility

CLAIRE: You'll represent me then?

MISS HILL: Miss Harrison, I'll let you know my decision after I've seen Dr. Emerson.

CLAIRE: But you will come back and tell me your decision yourself, even if Dr. Emerson convinces you he's right?

MISS HILL: I'll come back.

CLAIRE: He'll try the heavy father bit with his wayward daughter.

MISS HILL: So does my senior partner. He doesn't get anywhere with it either.

She makes to go out then pauses to place her briefcase on the side cabinet. She smiles at CLAIRE.

CLAIRE: Miss Hill, if anyone tries to steal that, I'll … I'll … swear horribly at them.

MISS HILL *walks to* SISTER'S *office and* SISTER ANDERSON *takes her out to find* DR. EMERSON. *Fade up on downstage area.* KAY *enters with tray.* JOHN *enters with dead body completely covered on a trolley.*

JOHN: Kay! Kay! Wait … I want to talk to you …
(TO DEAD BODY) Stay there. Don't move.
(BACK TO KAY) Now, why won't you go out with me?

KAY: It's just that I'm so busy …

JOHN: All work and no play … makes for a boring day.

KAY: John, I hardly know you.

JOHN: Right … that's why I want to take you out … to find out what goes on behind those blue eyes …

KAY: At the present, there's just lists of bones and organs, all getting jumbled up.

5 **convince sb. sth.**: make sb. believe that sth. is true 7 **heavy**: (here) strict **wayward**: out of control 8 **senior partner**: lawyer in charge of a law firm **get anywhere**: (here) have success 26 **jumbled up**: confused

JOHN: Because you're working too hard …

KAY: Ask me next week …

JOHN: Okay. It's a deal …

KAY: Right!

JOHN: And I'll ask you this afternoon as well.

KAY *exits.* JOHN *turns back to the body. He puts his finger to his lips.*

JOHN (CONT'D): Sh! … Don't tell a soul.

JOHN *exits pushing the body.*

Cross Fade on DR. EMERSON'S *room.* DR. EMERSON *and* MISS HILL *enter his office.*

DR. EMERSON: Come into my office, Miss Hill. We can talk in here.

MISS HILL: Thank you, Dr. Emerson.

DR. EMERSON: You've seen Miss Harrison?

MISS HILL: Yes.

DR. EMERSON: It's a real tragedy. Such an attractive, talented woman. I do hope you'll be able to get enough money for her … she deserves everything we can get.

MISS HILL: Dr. Emerson, it's not about that I wanted to see you. I thought I was coming about that, but Miss Harrison wishes to retain me to represent her on quite another matter.

DR. EMERSON: Oh?

MISS HILL: She wants to be discharged.

DR. EMERSON: That's impossible.

MISS HILL: Why?

3 **it's a deal**: I accept 20 **retain (a lawyer)**: employ a lawyer to represent you

DR. EMERSON: To put it bluntly, she would die if we did that.

MISS HILL: She knows that. It's what she wants.

DR. EMERSON: And you are asking me to kill my patient?

MISS HILL: I am representing Miss Harrison's wishes to you and asking you to discharge her.

DR. EMERSON: I can't

They look at each other.

MISS HILL: Are we talking medicine or ethics here?

DR. EMERSON: Miss Hill, this is absurd …

MISS HILL: You can, of course, dismiss me like that if you choose, but I would hardly think it serves anyone's interests, least of all Miss Harrison's.

DR. EMERSON: I am trying to save her life. There is no need to remind me of my duty to my patient, Miss Hill.

MISS HILL: Or mine to my client, Dr. Emerson.

DR. EMERSON: Are you telling me that you have accepted the job of coming to me to urge a course of action that will lose your client her life?

MISS HILL: I hadn't accepted it … no … I told Miss Harrison I would talk to you first. Now I have, and I begin to see why she thought it necessary to be represented.

DR. EMERSON: … All right … Let's start again … Now tell me what you want to know.

MISS HILL: Miss Harrison wishes to be discharged from hospital. Will you make the necessary arrangements?

DR. EMERSON: No.

1 **bluntly**: in clear language 10 **dismiss**: *ablehnen* 17 **urge**: recommend **course of action**: sequence of activities

MISS HILL: May I ask why not?

DR. EMERSON: Because she is incapable of living outside the hospital and it is my duty as a doctor to preserve life.

MISS HILL: I take it that Miss Harrison is a voluntary patient here.

DR. EMERSON: Of course.

MISS HILL: Then I fail to see the legal basis for your refusal.

DR. EMERSON: Please, can't you understand? She is suffering from depression. She is incapable of making a rational decision about her life and death.

MISS HILL: Are you maintaining that she is mentally unbalanced?

DR. EMERSON: … Yes.

MISS HILL: Would you have any objection to my bringing in a psychiatrist for a second opinion?

DR. EMERSON: Of course not, but why not ask the consultant psychiatrist here? I'm sure he will be able to convince you.

MISS HILL: Oh. He's examined Miss Harrison?

DR. EMERSON (REACHING FOR THE TELEPHONE): No, but that can be quickly arranged.

MISS HILL: That's very kind of you, Dr. Emerson, but I'm sure you'll understand if I ask for my own – whose opinion you are not sure of before he examines the patient.

DR. EMERSON: … Good afternoon, Miss Hill.

MISS HILL: Good afternoon.

She exits and walks around to CLAIRE'S *room.*

3 **preserve**: *bewahren* 6 **legal basis**: *gesetzliche Grundlage* 10 **maintain**: (here) say **mentally unbalanced**: not in a position to make a rational decision

DR. EMERSON (PICKING UP THE TELEPHONE): Could you find out where Dr. Jacobs is, please? I want to see him urgently, and put me through to the Chief Executive. Well, put me through when he's free and send in Dr. Scott will you?

Cross Fade on CLAIRE'S *room.* MISS HILL *comes in.*

CLAIRE: So, how was it on Mount Olympus?

MISS HILL: Cloudy.

CLAIRE: No joy then?

MISS HILL: Dr. Emerson does not want to discharge you.

CLAIRE: Surprise, surprise. So what do we do now?

MISS HILL: Miss Harrison, I will be perfectly frank. Dr. Emerson claims that you are not in a sufficiently healthy mental state to make a rational decision, especially one of this seriousness and finality. Now, my position is I am not competent to decide whether or not he is right.

CLAIRE: So how will you decide?

MISS HILL: I would like to have you examined by an independent psychiatrist and I will accept his view of the case and advise you accordingly.

CLAIRE: Fair enough. Will Emerson agree?

MISS HILL: He has already.

CLAIRE: All right, that's a beginning …

MISS HILL: I have to warn you that Dr. Emerson is likely to take steps to have you admitted here under the Mental Health Act as mentally unbalanced. This means that he can keep you here and give you any treatment he sees fit.

2 **urgently**: *dringend* 2–3 **put sb. through to sb. else**: *jdn. an jdn. weiterverbinden*
8 **no joy** (infml): no luck 11 **frank**: honest 14 **finality** [faɪ'næləti]: *Endgültigkeit*
19 **accordingly**: as the circumstances suggest 26 **fit**: (here) appropriate

CLAIRE: My God. Can he do that?

MISS HILL: He probably can.

CLAIRE: And I have no say in it?

MISS HILL: Oh, yes. He will need another signature and that doctor will be a psychiatrist trained in the Mental Health Act. He will also need the agreement of an approved Social Worker.

CLAIRE: Ah! That'll be Mrs. Boyle, I bet. He won't have any problem there.

MISS HILL: Even if he gets both we can still appeal.

CLAIRE: Let's get on with it then.

MISS HILL: One thing at a time. First, you remember, our own psychiatrist.

CLAIRE: Wheel him in …

MISS HILL: I'll be in touch soon then.

CLAIRE: Oh, before you go. The other day I refused to take a tranquilizer and Emerson came in and gave me an injection. It made me pretty dopey. If I were like that when the psychiatrist came he'd lock me up for life!

MISS HILL: He can't do that again unless he admits you under the Mental Health Act. But I'll make sure you'll be fully awake for the assessment. Good-bye for now then.

CLAIRE: Good bye

MISS HILL *exits. Cross fade on* DR. EMERSON'S *office.* DR. SCOTT *enters.*

DR. SCOTT: You wanted to see me?

DR. EMERSON: Yes. Claire Harrison's decided to discharge herself.

DR. SCOTT: Oh, no. Well, I'm not surprised.

9 **appeal**: ask to have a decision changed 17 **dopey**: sleepy and stupid
19 **admit**: (here) keep sb. in hospital

DR. EMERSON: So, Jacobs is seeing her now.

DR. SCOTT: Dr. Jacobs won't make her change her mind.

DR. EMERSON: I am committing her under the Mental Health Act.

DR. SCOTT: Oh. Will Dr. Jacobs sign it?

DR. EMERSON: Of course he will.

DR. SCOTT: It may not be so easy. I can name you many psychiatrists who wouldn't take a suicide attempt as evidence of insanity.

DR. EMERSON: I could name you several psychiatrists who are evidence of insanity … I have no choice. Don't you see, David? She's got herself a solicitor. It's the only way I can keep her here.

DR. SCOTT: Are you sure you should?

DR. EMERSON: Of course. No question.

DR. SCOTT: It's her life.

DR. EMERSON: But my responsibility.

DR. SCOTT: Only if she's incapable of making her own decision.

DR. EMERSON: But she isn't capable. I refuse to believe that a woman with a mind as quick as hers, with enormous mental resources, would calmly choose suicide.

DR. SCOTT: But she has, she's done just that.

DR. EMERSON: And, therefore, I say she is unbalanced.

DR. SCOTT: But surely a wish to die is not necessarily a symptom of insanity? A person might want to die for perfectly sane reasons.

DR. EMERSON: No, David. A doctor cannot accept the choice for death. He's committed to life. When a patient is brought into my unit, he's in a bad way. I don't stand around wondering whether

7 **suicide**: the act of killing yourself **insanity**: madness 17 **quick**: (here) clever **mental resources**: intelligence 22 **sane**: sensible and reasonable 25 **in a bad way**: unhealthy, ill

or not it's worth saving his life. I haven't the time for doubts, I get in there, do whatever I can to save life. I can't function in any other way. I'm a doctor, not a judge.

DR. SCOTT: I hope you'll forgive me for asking this, but isn't that exactly how you're behaving – as a judge?

DR. EMERSON: You must, of course, say what you think – but I am the responsible person here.

DR. SCOTT: I know that.

DR. SCOTT *makes to go.*

DR. EMERSON: … David, don't treat me as your enemy. There's only one enemy here, Death. If anyone in my unit dies before his allotted three score years and ten then the bastard's won! I'm not stupid, David. I know we can't win 'em all but I'll never lose willingly.

DR. SCOTT: No, Sir.

DR. EMERSON: … Claire Harrison is now physically stable. There is no reason why she should die. If she should die suddenly, I would think it necessary to order a post-mortem and to act on whatever was found.

DR. SCOTT: … Claire Harrison is your patient, sir.

DR. EMERSON (SMILING): Of course, of course. You make that sound a fate worse than death.

DR. SCOTT: Perhaps for her it is.

DR. SCOTT *exits. Cross Fade on* CLAIRE'S *room.* DR. EMERSON *crosses around to CLAIRE'S room. He enters.*

DR. EMERSON: Miss Harrison, we seem to have got off on the wrong foot.

9 **make to go**: act as if you're about to leave 12 **allotted**: given 12 **score**: twenty ($3 \times 20 + 10 = 70$) 18 **post-mortem**: examination of a dead body to find the cause of death 22 **fate**: *Schicksal* 26–27 **get off on the wrong foot**: start a relationship badly

CLAIRE: Dr. Emerson, whatever else you can say about me, that is one charge that is patently ridiculous.

DR. EMERSON *thinks then sees his mistake and laughs. Then shakes his head in admiration.*

DR. EMERSON: You are very funny.

CLAIRE: Really? Perhaps the laughter is put on, to put me at my ease, so you can manipulate me … Or does that sound like paranoia?

DR. EMERSON: Would you describe yourself as suffering from paranoia?

CLAIRE: No.

DR. EMERSON: What would you say paranoia was?

CLAIRE: Difficult. It depends on the person. Someone whose feelings of security are tied to his or her sense of what is right and will accept no denial. If the person were, say, a sculptor, then we would describe the condition as paranoia. If, however, he were a doctor, we would describe it as professionalism.

DR. EMERSON (LAUGHING): You don't like doctors!

CLAIRE: Do you like patients?

DR. EMERSON: Some.

CLAIRE: I like some doctors.

DR. EMERSON: What's wrong with the other doctors then?

CLAIRE: There are some who dole out information like a kosher butcher doles out pork sausages, and others that will tell you everything you want to know but deep down they know, you just don't have the mental equipment or training to use that knowledge.

2 **charge**: accusation **patently**: without doubt 6 **put on**: not real 6–7 **put sb. at their ease**: make sb. feel comfortable 23 **dole sth. out**: give sth.

DR. EMERSON: That's probably fair. But you'd agree that patients need medical knowledge to make good decisions?

CLAIRE: I would. Look at me, for example. An airy-fairy artist with no capability of understanding anything about my own body. It just so happens that I could probably hold my own with you in a competition in anatomy.

DR. EMERSON: It's a long time since I did any formal anatomy.

CLAIRE: Whereas I was teaching it every day up until five months ago. It wouldn't be fair.

DR. EMERSON: Your knowledge of anatomy may be excellent, but what's your neurology like? Or your dermatology, endocrinology, urology and so on?

CLAIRE: Lousy. And in so far as these bear on my case, I should be grateful for information so that I can make a proper decision. What I get from Doctors are decisions not information. I've learned more from my boyfriend's trawling the internet than I have from doctors … Suppose you came to my studio to buy something. You looked at all my pieces and you said, "I want the mother and child" and I said, "No, no, no. You don't know anything about sculpture; the proportion's all wrong, the texture's boring … You are having the flamingo!" You'd think I was crazy. You might ask for my professional opinion but as a mature adult, you'd reserve the right to choose for yourself.

DR. EMERSON: But we're not talking about a piece of sculpture to decorate a room, but about your life.

CLAIRE: That's right. My life.

3 **air-fairy** (infml): not practical 11 **neurology**: study of the nervous system **dermatology**: study of the skin **endocrinology**: study of the hormones 12 **urology**: study of the urinary system 13 **lousy** (infml): bad 14 **grateful** [greɪtfl]: *dankbar* 16 **trawl** (infml): search 22 **mature**: *reif*

DR. EMERSON: But your obvious intelligence weakens your case. I'm not saying that you would find life easy, but you do have resources that an unintelligent person doesn't have.

CLAIRE: My God, Catch 22. If you're clever and sane enough to put up an invincible case for suicide it demonstrates you ought not to die.

DR. EMERSON *moves to the stool near the bed and straightens it.*

CLAIRE (CONT'D): That's a nasty little tidiness compulsion you've got there.

DR. EMERSON (WRYLY): I was an only child … Have you any relationships outside the hospital?

CLAIRE: No, I don't get around much.

DR. EMERSON: You're not married I see.

CLAIRE: I was. I married young. It didn't work out.

DR. EMERSON: I see … Any other relationships?

CLAIRE: I was living with a man when this happened.

DR. EMERSON: Oh yes, I remember. A very handsome chap. He visits you often doesn't he?

CLAIRE: He did. He was very good … Two weeks ago I told him I didn't want to see him again.

DR. EMERSON: He must have been upset.

CLAIRE: Better than a lifetime's sacrifice.

DR. EMERSON: He wanted to … stay with you then?

4 **Catch 22**: title of a war novel (1961) by Joseph Heller (if a pilot was sane, he had to fly into battle; if he put up a case for not flying, he proved he was sane and had to fly) 5 **invincible**: too strong to be defeated 8 **tidiness compulsion**: *zwanghaftes Bedürfnis nach Ordnung* 12 **get around** (infml): (here) go out socially 22 **sacrifice**: *Aufopferung*

CLAIRE: Oh, yes … Had it all worked out … But he's a healthy man. He should have a baby, a real one. Not one that will never learn to walk.

DR. EMERSON: But if that's what he really wants.

CLAIRE: Oh, come on, Doctor. If that's what he really wants, there are plenty of other cripples out there who want help. I told him to go, to release him, I hope, from the guilt he would feel if he did what he really wanted to.

DR. EMERSON: That's very generous.

CLAIRE: No, no. I did it for me. It would destroy my self respect if I allowed myself to become the object with which people could safely exploit their masochistic tendencies.

DR. EMERSON: That's putting it very strongly.

CLAIRE: Yes. Too strongly. But you're beginning to sound like the chaplain. He was in here the other day. He seemed to think I should be perfectly happy to be God's chosen vessel into which people could pour their compassion … I'm fed up with those religious people who believe their God can tell me what I can do. I do what my God tells me to do.

DR. EMERSON: You do have a God then.

CLAIRE: … The jury's out on that one. But if I do, He's a God of compassion and toleration.

DR. EMERSON: … What about your parents? Are they living?

CLAIRE: In New York. I thought it would break my mother – I always thought of my father as very tough. Typical working class. But it was the other way around. My father can think only with his hands. He used to stand around here, completely at a loss. My

6 **cripple** (sl): disabled person 12 **exploit**: (here) use **masochistic**: enjoying the experience of being hurt 15 **chaplain**: priest 16 **vessel**: *Gefäß* 21 **the jury's out**: no decision has been made 25 **tough**: (here) not emotional 27 **at a loss**: not knowing what to do

mother would sit there – just understanding. They were here a week ago – I got rid of my father for a while and told my mother what I was going to do. She looked at me for a minute. There were tears in her eyes. She said. "… it's your life … don't worry about your dad – I'll get him over it." … She stood up and I said, "What about you?" "What about me?" she said, "You're your own woman. I'm proud of you. Always was. Always will be … ."
(TEARS ARE VERY CLOSE)
… I'd like to think I am my mother's daughter.

DR. EMERSON: Yes, well, we'll have to see …

CLAIRE: You mean you haven't made up your mind yet?

DR. EMERSON: I'd like to do some tests …

CLAIRE: What tests, for God's sake? I can tell you right now, my time over a hundred metres is lousy.

DR. EMERSON: You seem very angry.

CLAIRE: Yes, I am. But I am trying to hold it in – otherwise you'll just write me off as being in the manic phase of a manic-depressive cycle.

DR. EMERSON: You are very free with psychiatric jargon.

CLAIRE: Oh, well then, you'll be able to write me off as an obsessive hypochondriac.

DR. EMERSON: I certainly wouldn't do that, Miss Harrison.

CLAIRE: Can't you see what a trap I'm in? How the hell can anyone prove that they're sane? Could you?

DR. EMERSON: I'll come and see you again.

2 **get rid of sb.** (infml): send sb. away 5 **get sb. over sth.**: help sb. to accept sth. 17 **write sb. off**: dismiss sb. 17–18 **manic-depressive cycle**: alternating periods of extreme excitement and desperation 20 **obsessive**: *obsessiv* 21 **hypochondriac** [haɪpəˈkɒndriæk]: *Hypochonder* 23 **trap**: situation you can't escape from

CLAIRE: No, don't come and see me again, because the more you come the more you'll make me angry, and frustrated and depressed. And eventually you will destroy my mind.

DR. EMERSON: I'm sorry if I upset you.

CLAIRE: Please, just leave me alone.

DR. EMERSON *replaces the stool and moves to the door.*

DR. EMERSON: … I'll take your professional advice, Claire. I'll have the flamingo … But what interests me, is why is the Mother and Child still in your studio in that terrible state? I couldn't tolerate the evidence of failure. I'd have to work at it till it was right … I can't let you go, Claire. Like you, I'm a professional.

DR. EMERSON *goes out.*

Cross Fade

DR. SCOTT *and* MISS HILL *in outdoor clothes. It is late evening and they've just been out for dinner.*

DR. SCOTT: I hate it. I hate the whole idea. It's against all my training and instincts …

MISS HILL: Mine too. But we're not talking about euthanasia here, are we?

DR. SCOTT: Something very close.

MISS HILL: No. Something very far away. Suicide.

DR. SCOTT: Thank you for a lovely dinner.

MISS HILL: I'm glad you accepted. Tell me, what would you think – or rather feel – if there were a miracle and Claire Harrison were granted the use of her hands for just one minute and she used it to grab a bottle of sleeping pills and swallowed them all?

DR. SCOTT: It's irrational but … I'd be very … relieved.

18 **euthanasia**: *Sterbehilfe* 26 **grab sth.**: take sth. suddenly with your hands

MISS HILL: It wouldn't go against your instincts … ? You wouldn't feel it was a wasted life and fight with stomach pumps and all that?

DR. SCOTT: No … not if it were my decision.

MISS HILL: You might even be sure there was a bottle of pills handy and you not there.

DR. SCOTT: You make it harder and harder … but, yes, I might even do that …

MISS HILL: Yes. Perhaps we ought to make suicide respectable again. Whenever anyone kills himself there's a whole legal rigmarole to go through – investigations, inquests and so on – and it all seems designed to find someone or something to blame. Can you ever recall a Coroner saying something like "We've heard all the evidence of how the deceased was facing literally insurmountable odds and he made a courageous decision. I record a verdict of a noble death."?

DR. SCOTT: No … Well, I don't know if I've been of any use to you.

MISS HILL: You have. I've made up my mind.

DR. SCOTT: You'll help her?

MISS HILL: Yes … I hope you're not sorry.

DR. SCOTT: … No …

MISS HILL: I'm sure it is morally wrong for anyone to try to hand the responsibility for his or her death to anyone else. But Claire isn't trying to do that.

DR. SCOTT: I'm glad you've made up your mind …

2 **stomach pump** ['stʌmək pʌmp]: *Magenpumpe* 5 **handy**: (here) nearby 10 **legal rigmarole** ['rɪgmərəʊl]: long and complicated legal process 11 **inquest**: *gerichtliche Untersuchung* 12 **designed**: made especially 14 **deceased**: (here) dead person 14–15 **insurmountable odds** [ˌɪnsə'maʊntəbl]: difficulties which cannot be solved 16 **noble**: *großmütig* 22 **hand** (v): give 25 **make up your mind**: make a decision

He doesn't really want to go. HELEN *offers her hand.* SCOTT *takes it.*

DR. SCOTT (CONT'D): I hope I see you again.

MISS HILL: I'm on the phone … Good night, David.

DR. SCOTT: Good night, Helen.

She exits. DR. SCOTT *thinks for a moment and leaves.*

Cross Fade to CLAIRE'S room. KAY enters carrying a dinner tray.

CLAIRE: You still on duty?

KAY (SNAPPING AT HER): We're very short staffed …

She puts a napkin on CLAIRE.

CLAIRE: Why are there no bunny rabbits on my bib?

KAY: I'm sorry.

CLAIRE: That's all right.

KAY: It looks good tonight … mince.

CLAIRE: Excellent … and what wine shall we order then? How about a '48 claret? Yes, I think so. Send for the wine waiter.

KAY *laughs.*

KAY: You're crazy!

CLAIRE: Oh God! Have you signed the bloody form too?

KAY *is puzzled.*

CLAIRE (CONT'D): Is there any reason why I shouldn't have wine?

KAY: I don't know. I'll ask Sister if you want me to.

CLAIRE: I wouldn't bother. They do seem determined to depress my consciousness but they'd think it was immoral if I enjoyed it.

3 **on the phone**: (here) able to be contacted by phone 8 **be short staffed**: not have enough people to do all the work 10 **bib**: *Lätzchen* 13 **mince**: *Hackfleisch* 15 **claret**: type of red wine

KAY *gives her a spoonful of dinner.*

CLAIRE (CONT'D): It's a bit salty.

KAY: Do you want some water?

CLAIRE: That would be very good.

She sips the water.

CLAIRE (CONT'D): Very nice … not too full of body. Chateau Ogston Reservoir, I think, with just a cheeky little hint of Jeyes fluid from the steriliser.

KAY: We use Milton.

CLAIRE: Oh dear … the final catastrophe. Claire Harrison's palate is failing. Rush up the taste resuscitation unit … "Nurse, give me orange … no response … quick the lemon … God! Not a flicker … we're on a tightrope … Nurse, pass the ultimate … quick! There's no time to lose! Pass the hospital mince! That brings people back from the dead!" Don't tell Emerson.

KAY *offers more food.*

KAY: Come on.

CLAIRE: I don't want any more.

KAY: Are you sure?

CLAIRE: Positive. Just in case I'm right.

KAY: Would you like some more water?

CLAIRE: Oh, yes, please, since they've gone to all the trouble of heating it up.

6 **full of body**: used to describe wine with strong flavours 6–7 **Ogston Reservoir** [ˈrezəvwɑː]: *Reservoir in England* 7 **cheeky** (infml): (here) refreshing **hint**: *Anzeichen* **Jeyes/Milton fluid**: brands of cleaning fluid 10 **palate**: *Gaumen* 11 **resuscitation**: *Wiederbelebung* 12 **flicker**: (here) small sign of life 13 **on a tightrope**: in a critical situation

She takes a sip. KAY *puts the drink on the side table, then lets the bed down.*

CLAIRE (CONT'D): Did you hear about the plastic surgeon who melted in front of the fire?

KAY: No.

She gets the joke and laughs.

CLAIRE: You get there in the end, don't you?

KAY: Yes, finally.

KAY *turns* CLAIRE *on her side and props her with pillows, settling her for the night.*

CLAIRE: Got time for another one?

KAY: Oh, yes please.

CLAIRE: A carrot is out for a walk and he's knocked down by an onion driving a jag. When the carrot wakes up in hospital he asks the surgeon, "Will I be all right?" And the surgeon says, "Yes, but you'll be vegetable for the rest of your life."

Beat.

CLAIRE (CONT'D): Do you know what you do with a dog that has no legs?

KAY: No. What?

CLAIRE: You take it for a drag.

KAY: That's terrible.

She gathers the tray and starts to go.

CLAIRE: Good night, Flea.

KAY: Good night.

14 **jag**: *Jaguar* (sports car) 21 **drag**: *zerren*

She exits.

DR. SCOTT *enters and walks by* CLAIRE'S *room. He sees her light and enters.*

CLAIRE (HEARING HIM): Sister?

DR. SCOTT: No, it's me. Still awake?

CLAIRE: Yes.

DR. SCOTT: It's late.

CLAIRE: What time is it?

DR. SCOTT: Half past eleven.

CLAIRE: I can't sleep. I want to think.

DR. SCOTT: Yes.

CLAIRE: You look very handsome.

DR. SCOTT: Thank you.

CLAIRE: Have you been out?

DR. SCOTT: For dinner.

CLAIRE: Nice. Good company?

DR. SCOTT: You're fishing.

CLAIRE: That's right.

DR. SCOTT: Yes, it was good company.

CLAIRE: A colleague?

DR. SCOTT: No. Actually, it was Helen Hill, your solicitor.

CLAIRE: Well, well, well … it didn't take her long to get going, did it?

17 **fish**: (here) try to find out private information

DR. SCOTT: It was just a dinner.

CLAIRE: I know I asked her to act for me. I just didn't realise she would see her duties so comprehensively.

DR. SCOTT: It was just a dinner!

CLAIRE: I hope my surrogate self behaved myself?

DR. SCOTT: You were a perfect lady.

CLAIRE: Mmm … then perhaps I'd better engage another surrogate.

DR. SCOTT: Do you mind, really?

CLAIRE: No. Unless you convinced her that Emerson was right.

DR. SCOTT: … I didn't try.

CLAIRE: Thank you.

DR. SCOTT: I think you're enjoying all this.

CLAIRE: I am, in a way. I'll tell you, for the first time in months I feel like a human being again.

DR. SCOTT: Yes.

Pause.

DR. SCOTT: Isn't that the whole point, Claire? Isn't that what this fight has shown you? That you are a human being again? You're not fighting for death. I don't want to believe that you really want to win.

CLAIRE: That was what I had to think about.

DR. SCOTT: And have you … changed your mind?

CLAIRE: … No. I know I'm enjoying the fight and I had to be sure that I wanted to win, really get what I'm fighting for, and not just doing it to convince myself I'm still alive.

DR. SCOTT: And are you sure?

3 **comprehensively**: completely, thoroughly 5 **surrogate self**: *Ersatz-Ich*

CLAIRE: Yes. Could you do something about this pillow?

DR. SCOTT *adjusts the pillow. They look at each other.*

CLAIRE (CONT'D): Oh, David, for me life is over. I can't say what I want to say, and I can't do anything I want to do, so it had better end. You understand, don't you?

DR. SCOTT *nods his head.*

CLAIRE (CONT'D): So, tomorrow, on with the fight!

DR. SCOTT: Good night …

CLAIRE: Good night … David?

DR. SCOTT: Yes?

CLAIRE: Are you driving home?

DR. SCOTT: Yes.

CLAIRE: Use your seat belt, huh?

DR. SCOTT *nods and exits.*

Lights change to morning. MISS HILL *enters. As she passes Sister Anderson's office the Sister emerges.*

SISTER ANDERSON: Good morning, Miss Hill.

MISS HILL: Good morning, Sister. How is she today?

SISTER ANDERSON: Very well.

MISS HILL: Good.

She makes to go to the ward.

SISTER ANDERSON: Have you asked Dr. Emerson if you can visit her?

MISS HILL: … My office informed him that I was coming. He made no objection. You can check with him if you wish.

13 **seat belt**: *Sicherheitsgurt*

SISTER ANDERSON: That won't be necessary. However, Dr. Emerson has asked that I or a qualified nurse be present whenever you interview her.

MISS HILL: Why?

SISTER ANDERSON: We're very worried about her mental condition, as you know. Her breathing function can't cope with emotional stress, so Dr. Emerson has ordered that someone must be there as a precaution.

MISS HILL: I see … Very well.

SISTER ANDERSON: This way, please.

They go into CLAIRE'S *room.*

SISTER ANDERSON (CONT'D): A visitor for you, Claire.

CLAIRE: Morning Helen.

MISS HILL: Morning Claire. Dr. Emerson has insisted that Sister Anderson remains during my stay. Evidently you might get too excited.

CLAIRE *smiles.*

CLAIRE: Ooh! Well, Miss Hill is a very attractive woman, Sister, but she doesn't turn me on. Does she you? Is this a new side of our cool and collected sister?

MISS HILL *has to hide a grin.* SISTER ANDERSON *purses her lips as she moves to the bed side and reaches under the sheets.*

CLAIRE (CONT'D): Sister Anderson, what are you doing … ?

SISTER ANDERSON *takes* CLAIRE'S *wrist to take her pulse.*

CLAIRE (CONT'D): Oh, I see. Just for a moment there I didn't know what she was after.

8 **precaution** [prɪˈkɔːʃn]: *Sicherheitsmaßnahme* 15 **evidently**: obviously 19 **turn sb. on**: make sb. sexually excited 20 **cool and collected**: calm and sensible
21 **purse your lips**: *die Lippen kräuseln*

Beat.

CLAIRE (CONT'D): Sixteen, seventeen …

SISTER: You mustn't … .

CLAIRE: Twenty-two … Thirty-nine.

SISTER *gives up trying to take her pulse.*

SISTER: Very well.

SISTER *moves to the side of the ward away from* MISS HILL.

CLAIRE: So today's the day you said you'd make up your mind if you'd represent me.

MISS HILL: Yes … I've now received all of the psychiatric reports.

CLAIRE: And?

MISS HILL: The hospital's psychiatrist still insists you're not yet capable of making the decision but he does say that he would need to review this in a few months.

CLAIRE: But what of my psychiatrist?

MISS HILL *produces some sheets of paper from her briefcase.*

MISS HILL: Here is his report. He says he can understand the hospital's fighting to save their patient from herself, but no matter how much he sympathises with them and how much he wishes he could get her to change her mind, nevertheless, she is sane and knows exactly what she is doing and why she is doing it.

CLAIRE: Oh! Thank God for that. So, you'll represent me? Do whatever you have to do to get me out of here?

MISS HILL *paces at the foot of the bed, thinking.*

MISS HILL: … If you succeed in your aim, without water you will be dead within days.

6 **very well** (fml): (here) OK 10 **report**: *Bericht* 14 **review**: examine again
18–19 **no matter how much**: *egal wie viel*

CLAIRE: I know.

MISS HILL: I am informed that without a catheter the toxic substances will build up in your bloodstream and you will be slowly poisoned by your own blood.

CLAIRE: Do you always beat about the bush?

MISS HILL: I have to be sure you know what you are doing.

CLAIRE: I know.

MISS HILL: And you have no doubts whatsoever … no reservations?

CLAIRE: None at all.

MISS HILL *relaxes with a slight smile.*

MISS HILL: Let's look at the possibilities. You are now being held under the Mental Health Act which means they can keep you here and give you any treatment they believe you need. Under the law we can appeal to a tribunal.

CLAIRE: How long will that take?

MISS HILL: In 2002, some patients won an appeal because the court held that 27 weeks was too long to wait. So it could be under that.

CLAIRE: That's more than six months. Can't it be quicker than that?

MISS HILL: Not much I should think.

CLAIRE: I'm ready now. It's cruel to make me wait.

A long pause. MISS HILL *thinks.*

MISS HILL: I've thought about this. I'm inclined to try Habeas Corpus …

2 **toxic**: poisonous, deadly 5 **beat about the bush**: be unclear 8 **reservation**: feeling of doubt 14 **tribunal**: type of court 17 **hold** (fml): (here) decide
23–24 **Habeas Corpus**: law that a person cannot be kept (usually in jail) for longer than a particular period of time

CLAIRE: Habeas Corpus? I thought that had something to do with criminals.

MISS HILL: It usually does. Briefly, it's against the law to deprive anyone of their liberty without proper cause. If anyone is so deprived, he or a friend can apply for a Writ of Habeas Corpus, which is Latin for "you may have the body."

CLAIRE: Particularly apt in my case.

MISS HILL: The people who are doing the detaining have to produce the ... person before the judge and if they can't give a good enough reason for keeping him, the judge will order that he be released.

CLAIRE: How long will it take?

MISS HILL: Habeas Corpus is one of the very few legal processes that move very fast. We can approach any judge at any time and he will see that it's heard quickly.

CLAIRE: Will I have to go to court?

MISS HILL: Probably not. If he ordered you to be produced in court and anything happened to you, it would be a classic case of pre-judging the issue.

CLAIRE: I wouldn't mind.

MISS HILL: But the judge might feel rather foolish.

CLAIRE: But I want my day in court.

MISS HILL: It's much easier these days. We can establish a video link from here to the court. And the judge can visit you here.

CLAIRE: Thank you. It'll be an unusual case for you – making a plea for the defendant's death.

MISS HILL: I'll be honest with you. It's a case I could bear to lose.

3–4 **deprive sb of sth.**: prevent sb. from having sth. 21 **foolish** ['fu:lɪʃ]: stupid
25 **plea**: *Einspruch* 27 **bear** (v): (here) accept

CLAIRE: If you do, it's a life sentence for me.

MISS HILL: Well, we'll see.

MISS HILL *goes to* CLAIRE *and puts her hand out to offer a hand shake, realises, then covers Claire's hand with hers.*

Goodbye, Claire.

CLAIRE: Goodbye.

MISS HILL: See you soon.

She goes out with SISTER ANDERSON. *They pause downstage.*

MISS HILL (CONT'D): Sister … I'm very sorry about all this. I do realise it must be upsetting for you.

SISTER: Whereas for you, pulling off a legal coup would be very exciting.

MISS HILL: Do you really think that's what I'm doing? I hate it. I wish she'd make the opposite decision. You mustn't make assumptions about lawyers, Sister,

SISTER: Nor you about nurses, Miss Hill.

MISS HILL: You mean you think she's making the right decision?

SISTER: I am a professional too, Miss Hill. It would be inappropriate for me to offer an opinion in this case.

She turns and goes into her office, leaving a baffled MISS HILL *who slowly makes her way out.*

The next day CLAIRE *is listening to the Today Programme on Radio Four. A fixed video link camera is located in Claire's room.*

PRESENTER: Following yesterday's dramatic hearing in the High Court, Judge Dame Jane Millhouse, will today hear from Miss H

11 **coup** [ku:]: (here) impressive achievement 15 **assumption**: *Vermutung*
18 **inappropriate**: *unangemessen* 20 **baffled**: confused 24 **hearing**: *Gerichtsverhandlung*

directly at her bedside at the Crawthorne Hospital. Miss H watched the lawyers battle it out in the High Court yesterday on a television monitor in her room. Today she will have the opportunity to put her case for herself, that she be allowed to die.

JOHN *and* KAY *enter with chairs for the hearing.* JOHN *stops dead in his tracks when he sees the camera.*

JOHN: That … terrible woman …

CLAIRE: That's a little harsh. She looked a bit fierce yesterday on the video but I'm sure she'll be fair.

JOHN: I'm not talking about her! That's Sister Anderson's doing. That woman will stop at nothing to catch me sitting down.

KAY (GENTLY TEASING): John … !

JOHN: When this lady here has successfully topped herself, I will still be here with big sister watching my every move.

KAY (LAUGHING): You're crazy.

CLAIRE *picks up the changed vibes between the two.*

CLAIRE: Hey, hey, hey. What's going on here? Is Cupid playing fast and loose with his hypodermic?

KAY: No!

CLAIRE: John?

JOHN (TO THE CAMERA): Honestly, your honour, I'm not guilty. I was just walking down the corridor when I was struck dumb by the beauty of this nurse.

KAY: Don't be an idiot, John. We need an extra chair … Can you go and find one, please?

2 **battle it out**: fight 5–6 **stop dead in your tracks**: stop suddenly 8 **harsh**: unfair **fierce**: *kämpferisch* 13 **top yourself** (sl): commit suicide 16 **vibe**: atmosphere 17–18 **play fast and loose**: act irresponsibly 18 **hypodermic**: *Injektionsspritze* 22 **strike sb. dumb**: make sb. unable to speak

JOHN: Your wishes, oh queen, are my command.

He bows and goes out.

KAY: He is a fool.

CLAIRE: You've been out with him … haven't you? I'm sorry, that's none of my business … Well, have you?

KAY: We went to a concert of his last night … he plays in a band, you know.

CLAIRE: I know.

KAY: They're really good. They should go a long way. But I shouldn't be going on like this.

CLAIRE: Why not … ? Because I'm paralyzed? Because I can't go dancing? The other day John was in here and I was saying that I was useless, I served no purpose and all the rest of the whining miseries. John began finding things I could do. He said, because I could move my head from side to side …
(SHE DOES SO): I could be a tennis umpire. Then if I got really good, I'd move right on to ping-pong.
(SHE TURNS HER HEAD FASTER): I laughed so much that I thought they'd have to give me oxygen.

KAY: He is funny.

CLAIRE: He's more than that. He's free!

KAY: Free?

CLAIRE: Free of guilt. Almost everyone feels guilty about me – including you. That's why you didn't want to tell me what a great time you had dancing. So everybody makes me feel worse because I make them feel guilty. But not John. He's sorry for me, but he knows bloody well it isn't his fault. He's a tonic.

JOHN *comes back carrying* SISTER ANDERSON'S *armchair.*

9 **go a long way**: be successful 16 **umpire**: *Tennis-Schiedsrichter* 27 **tonic**: medicine which gives strength and energy

KAY: Did Sister say you could have that chair?

JOHN: She wasn't there.

JOHN *sits in the chair.*

KAY: She'll kill you; no one ever sits in her chair.

JOHN *jumps up in alarm.*

JOHN: Why? Is it contaminated or something? I just thought that if the poor old judge had to sit here listening to this misery guts moaning on about wanting to die, the least we could do was to make her comfortable.

CLAIRE (LAUGHING, TO KAY): See what I mean?

JOHN *sits in the chair and assumes a grave face.*

JOHN: Now this is a very serious case. The two charges are proved … Firstly, this hospital has been found guilty of using drugs to make people happy. A major crime. Next, and most surprising of all, this hospital, despite every effort to the contrary, is keeping people alive!

SISTER ANDERSON *comes in and catches* JOHN *sitting in her chair. He exits sheepishly under her glare.*

SISTER: That will be all, Nurse.

KAY *exits.*

CLAIRE: We have some very important visitors today.

SISTER: Indeed we have.

CLAIRE: Will you be here?

SISTER: No.

CLAIRE: I feel a bit like … a traitor.

6 **contaminated**: *kontaminiert* 7 **misery guts** (infml): sad person 8 **moan**: *lamentieren* 11 **grave**: serious 15 **contrary**: opposite 18 **sheepishly**: embarrassed 25 **traitor**: *Verräter*

SISTER: … We all do what we have to.

CLAIRE: But we don't all do it as well as you do.

SISTER (QUICKLY): Thank you.

She moves quickly to go. DR. SCOTT *comes in.*

DR. SCOTT: Good morning, Sister.

SISTER (BRIGHTLY): Good morning.

She exits. DR. SCOTT *enters* CLAIRE'S *room.*

CLAIRE: Damn …

DR. SCOTT: What?

CLAIRE: I've upset Sister, I'm afraid.

DR. SCOTT: You shouldn't do that. She's a marvellous Sister.

CLAIRE: That's what I told her.

DR. SCOTT: Oh. I see. Well, that's probably the one way past her defences. How are you this morning?

CLAIRE: Fine.

DR. SCOTT: And you're going ahead with it?

CLAIRE: Of course.

DR. SCOTT: Of course.

CLAIRE: I haven't had any pills, yesterday or today.

DR. SCOTT: No.

CLAIRE: Thank you.

DR. SCOTT: Don't thank me, thank the judge. She ordered it.

CLAIRE: Ah!

DR. EMERSON *comes in.*

DR. EMERSON: Good morning, Miss Harrison.

CLAIRE: Good morning.

DR. EMERSON: There's still time.

CLAIRE: No. I want to go on with it … unless you'll discharge me.

DR. EMERSON: I'm afraid I can't do that. The judge will be here soon. I thought I'd just stop by and see if you were all right. I should be grateful, Doctor, if you would remain here with Miss Harrison.

DR. SCOTT: Of course.

DR. EMERSON (SMILING): I wish you the best of luck, Miss Harrison – so that we'll be able to carry on treating you.

CLAIRE (SMILING): Thank you for your good wishes.

DR. EMERSON *nods and goes out.*

DR. SCOTT: If I didn't know you, I'd say he was the most obstinate person I've ever met.

As DR. EMERSON *makes for the* SISTER'S *office,* MISS HILL *comes down the corridor.*

MISS HILL: Good morning.

DR. EMERSON: Morning.

MISS HILL *stops and calls after* DR. EMERSON.

MISS HILL: Oh, Dr. Emerson …

DR. EMERSON: Yes?

MISS HILL: I just want to say how sorry I am that you have been forced into such a … distasteful situation.

DR. EMERSON: It's not over yet, Miss Hill. I have every confidence that the law is not such an ass that it will force me to watch a patient of mine die unnecessarily.

13 **obstinate**: stubborn 23 **distasteful**: unpleasant 25 **ass**: (here) idiot

MISS HILL: We are just as confident that the law is not such an ass that it will allow anyone arbitrary power.

DR. EMERSON: My power isn't arbitrary; I've earned it with knowledge and skill and it's also subject to the laws of nature.

MISS HILL: And to the laws of the state.

DR. EMERSON: If the state is so foolish as to believe it is competent to judge a purely professional issue.

MISS HILL: It's always doing that. Half the civil cases in the calendar arise because someone is challenging a professional's opinion.

DR. EMERSON: I don't know about other professions, but I do know this one. Medicine is being seriously threatened because of the intervention of law. Patients are becoming so litigious that doctors will soon be afraid to offer any opinion or take any action at all.

MISS HILL: Then they will be sued for negligence.

DR. EMERSON: We can't win.

MISS HILL (FOLLOWING HIM): Everybody wins. You wouldn't like to find yourself powerless in the hands of a lawyer, or a … bureaucrat. I wouldn't like to find myself powerless in the hands of a doctor.

DR. EMERSON: You make me sound as if I were some sort of Dracula …

MISS HILL: No! … I, for one, certainly don't doubt your good faith, but in spite of that I wouldn't like to place anyone above the law.

DR. EMERSON: I don't want to be above the law; I just want to be under laws that take full account of professional opinion.

MISS HILL: I'm sure it will do that, Dr. Emerson. The question is, whose professional opinion.

3 **arbitrary**: *willkürlich* 9 **arise**: *auftreten* 12 **intervention**: *Eingriff*
12 **litigious** [lɪˈtɪdʒəs]: too ready to take disagreements to court 14 **sue sb.**: *jmdn. verklagen* **negligence**: failure to give enough attention

DR. EMERSON: We shall see.

DR. EMERSON *exits.*

MISS HILL *goes into* CLAIRE'S *room. She goes up to* CLAIRE *and holds her hand.*

MISS HILL: Morning, Claire.

CLAIRE: Morning.

MISS HILL: Morning, Dr. Scott.

DR. SCOTT: Good morning. Big day.

MISS HILL: Indeed.
(TO CLAIRE): You're sure you …

CLAIRE: Yes! I'm absolutely sure. If I change my mind I'll announce it with a fanfare of trumpets. But please nobody hold their breath or everybody will die except me!

SISTER ANDERSON *enters with the* JUDGE.

SISTER: Mrs. Justice Millhouse.

They all rise.

JUDGE: Sit down, please … You are Claire Harrison?

CLAIRE: Yes.

The JUDGE *looks at her intently for a moment.*

JUDGE: This is a hearing held in informal circumstances. I wish to keep this hearing as brief as possible. You are, I take it, Dr. Scott.

DR. SCOTT: Yes, my lady.

JUDGE: I should be grateful, Doctor, if you would interrupt the proceedings any time you think it medically necessary.

DR. SCOTT: Yes, my lady.

19 **intently**: showing strong interest   21 **I take it**: as I understand it   23 **interrupt**: *unterbrechen*

JUDGE: Miss Harrison, you will have seen on the video link from the hearing in court yesterday that this case turns on whether or not you are in a sufficiently healthy mental state to make a decision that will inevitably lead to your death. You were able to follow the legal argument?

CLAIRE: Of course. I'm not simple-minded, let alone insane.

The JUDGE *looks at* CLAIRE *narrowly.*

JUDGE: Miss Harrison, I must ask you just to answer the questions. We are not here to decide if you are quick-witted but to decide if you are legally sane. Do you understand the distinction?

CLAIRE *bites back a retort.*

CLAIRE: Yes, Ma'am.

The JUDGE *refers to some papers.*

JUDGE: The psychiatric opinion is divided. Dr. Jacobs from this Hospital, believes Miss Harrison is suffering from an endogenous depression, that is to say she is clinically depressed to the point of mental illness …

CLAIRE: But I do want to be able to say what …

JUDGE (SHARPLY): Miss Harrison, this is, for the time being, no longer a hospital room but a court of law. You will conduct yourself accordingly. That means you will not interrupt proceedings at will. You will have your time to speak. Is that clear?

CLAIRE: Yes. I'm sorry.

The JUDGE *nods.*

JUDGE: The psychiatrist for the plaintiff, Dr. Travers from the Willingborough Hospital gave evidence that Miss Harrison's

2 **turn on sth.**: (here) depend on sth. 4 **inevitably**: definitely, certainly
6 **simple-minded**: stupid 9 **quick-witted**: clever 11 **retort**: answer
15 **endogenous** [en'dɒdʒənəs]: with no clear cause 21–22 **at will**: whenever you want 25 **plaintiff**: *Ankläger*

depression was reactive and entirely reasonable in the state of her physical health. I have decided to question Miss Harrison myself and both barristers have agreed that I can do so without their being present. But first I think it would be helpful to have evidence of Miss Harrison's general state at this time. Sister, would you ask Dr. Emerson to come in.

SISTER: Yes, my lady.

SISTER ANDERSON *goes to her office where* DR. EMERSON *is waiting.*

SISTER (CONT'D): Dr. Emerson, would you go in now, please.

DR. EMERSON: Thank you, Sister.

He goes into CLAIRE'S *room.*

JUDGE: Dr. Emerson. I would like you to take the oath.

The JUDGE *nods to her clerk who hands* DR. EMERSON *a bible and a card with the oath written on it.*

DR. EMERSON: I swear the evidence I give shall be the truth, the whole truth, and nothing but the truth.

JUDGE: You are Dr. Michael Emerson?

DR. EMERSON: I am.

JUDGE: And what is your position here?

DR. EMERSON: I am the consultant in charge of this unit.

JUDGE: Dr. Emerson, would you please give a brief account of your treatment of the patient?

DR. EMERSON (REFERRING TO NOTES): Miss Harrison was admitted here on the afternoon of October Ninth, as an emergency following a road accident. She was suffering from a fractured left tibia, right tibia and fibula, a fractured pelvis, four fractured ribs, one of which had punctured the lung, and a dislocated fourth

12 **oath**: *Eid* 26 **tibia**: bone in the leg 26 **fibula**: bone in the leg **pelvis**: *Becken* 27 **puncture**: *punktieren* **dislocated**: *ausgekugelt*

cervical vertebra, which had severed the spinal cord. She was extensively bruised and had minor lacerations. As a result of treatment, all the broken bones and ruptured tissue have healed with the exception of a severed spinal cord and this, together with the mental trauma, is now all that remains of the initial injury.

JUDGE: Precisely, Doctor. Let us deal with those last two points. Firstly, the spinal cord … Will there be any further improvement in that?

DR. EMERSON: In the present state of medical knowledge, I regret not, but there are many hopeful signs that at some stage, improvement may be possible.

JUDGE: Have you any idea when that might be possible?

DR. EMERSON: … No, my lady.

JUDGE: … And the mental trauma you spoke of?

DR. EMERSON: It's impossible to injure the body to the extent that Miss Harrison did and not affect the mind.

JUDGE: Thank you, Doctor.
(TO MISS HILL): Miss Hill, would you like to clear any points with Dr. Emerson?

MISS HILL: Doctor. Is there any objective way you could demonstrate this trauma? Are there, for example, the results of any tests or any measurements you can take to show it to us?

DR. EMERSON: No.

MISS HILL: Then how do you distinguish between a medical syndrome and a sane, even justified, depression?

1 **cervical vertebra**: *Halswirbel* **sever**: cut through 2 **extensively**: very **laceration**: *Risswunde* 3 **tissue**: *Gewebe* 5 **initial**: original 7 **precisely** [prɪ'saɪsli]: exactly 25 **distinguish**: see the difference

DR. EMERSON: By relying on the psychiatric report of a colleague I trust completely and of course, my experience as a physician, dealing with both types.

MISS HILL: No more questions, my lady.

JUDGE: Thank you, Dr. Emerson.

DR. EMERSON *nods and leaves.*

The JUDGE *stands and walks to* CLAIRE.

JUDGE (CONT'D): Do you feel like answering some questions?

CLAIRE: Of course.

JUDGE: Thank you.

CLAIRE: You are too kind.

JUDGE: Not at all.

CLAIRE: I mean it. I'd prefer it if you were a hanging judge.

JUDGE: There aren't any, any more.

CLAIRE: Society is now much more sensitive and humane?

JUDGE: You could put it that way.

CLAIRE: I'll settle for that.

JUDGE: I would like you to take the oath. Dr. Scott, her right hand please.

DR. SCOTT *places* CLAIRE'S *right hand on the Bible and holds the card for her to read.* CLAIRE *takes the oath.* DR. SCOTT *places her hand back under the sheets. The* JUDGE *sits.*

JUDGE (CONT'D): The Consultant Physician here has given evidence that you are not capable of making a rational decision.

CLAIRE: Yes, he's wrong.

15 **humane**: *menschlich* 16 **put it that way**: say it like that

JUDGE: How then do you think he came to that opinion?

CLAIRE: He's a good doctor and won't let a patient die if he can help it.

JUDGE: He found that you were suffering from acute depression.

CLAIRE: Is that surprising? I am completely paralyzed. I'd be insane if I weren't depressed.

JUDGE: But there is a difference between being unhappy and being clinically depressed.

CLAIRE: I thought that you said my psychiatrist had answered that point.

JUDGE: But, wishing to die …

CLAIRE: But my lady …

JUDGE: … must be strong evidence that depression has moved beyond mere unhappiness into a medical realm?

CLAIRE: My lady, I don't wish to die.

JUDGE: Then what is this case all about?

CLAIRE: As far as I'm concerned, I'm dead already. I just require the doctors to recognize that fact. I can't accept that this condition constitutes life in any real sense of the word.

JUDGE: Certainly, you're alive legally.

CLAIRE: I think I could challenge even that.

JUDGE: How?

CLAIRE: Any reasonable definition of life must include the idea of its being self-supporting. Hasn't it been decided in heart transplant cases that it's all right to take someone's heart if they require constant attention from respirators and so on to keep them alive?

4 **acute**: serious 14 **realm**: *Bereich* 19 **constitute sth.**: be considered as sth.
24 **self-supporting**: able to keep yourself alive 26 **respirator**: *Atemgerät*

JUDGE: There also has to be absolutely no brain activity at all. Yours is certainly working.

CLAIRE: Certainly and sanely.

JUDGE: That is the question to be decided.

CLAIRE: My lady, I am not asking anyone to kill me. I am only asking to be discharged from this hospital.

JUDGE: It comes to the same thing.

CLAIRE: Then that proves my point; not just that I will spend the rest of my life in a hospital, but that while I am there, everything is geared just to keeping my brain active, with no possibility of it ever being able to control anything. As far as I can see, that is an act of deliberate cruelty.

JUDGE: It might arguably be more cruel if society let people die, when it could, with some effort, keep them alive.

CLAIRE: No, not more cruel, just as cruel.

JUDGE: Then why should the hospital let you die – if it is just as cruel?

CLAIRE: Because the cruelty isn't a matter of saving someone or allowing them to die. It's that the choice is removed from the person concerned.

JUDGE: But a person who is very desperately depressed might not be capable of making a reasonable choice.

CLAIRE: As you said, My lady, that is the question to be decided.

JUDGE: All right. You tell me why it is a reasonable choice that you decided to die.

CLAIRE: … The best part of my life was, I suppose, my work. The most valuable asset that I had for that was my imagination. It's

10 **be geared to do sth.**: be focused on doing sth. 12 **deliberate** (adj): *absichtlich*
27 **asset**: *Vorzug*

just a shame that my mind wasn't paralyzed along with my body. Because my imagination – which was my most precious possession, has become my enemy. And it tortures me with thoughts of what might have been and of what might be to come. I can feel my mind slowly breaking up. For example, men. I loved what they were, the look of them, the way they thought, the smell of them … Now I dread it when they come into the room because I loathe the way they make me feel … You know, I am filled with absolute outrage that you, who have no connection with me whatever, has the right to condemn me to a life of torment because you can't see the pain. There's no blood and there's no screaming so you can't see it. But if you saw a mutilated animal on the side of the road, you'd shoot it. Well, I'm only asking that you show me the same mercy you'd show an animal. But I'm not asking you to commit an act of violence, just take me somewhere and leave me. And if you don't, then you come back here in five years and see what a piece of work you did today.

The JUDGE *stands up. She thinks a moment.*

JUDGE: This is a most unusual case. Before I give judgment, I want to state that I believe all the parties have acted in good faith. I propose to consider this matter for a moment.

The JUDGE *walks out into the corridor. She thinks for a while and returns. Those in the room rise. The* JUDGE *indicates that they sit. They do so.*

JUDGE (CONT'D): The law on this is fairly clear. A deliberate decision to embark on a course of action that will lead inevitably to death is not ipso facto evidence of insanity. If it were, society would have to reward many men with dishonourable burial rather than a posthumous medal for gallantry. On the other hand, we do have to bear in mind that Miss Harrison has suffered massive

7 **dread sth.**: be very afraid of sth. 8 **loathe**: hate 9 **outrage**: anger
10 **condemn sb.**: decide a punishment for sb. 11 **torment**: suffering
12 **mutilated**: badly damaged 14 **mercy**: *Gnade* 20 **act in good faith**: do what you think is right 25 **embark on sth.**: start doing sth. 26 **ipso facto**: because of the fact just mentioned

physical injuries and it is possible that her mind may have been affected. Any judge will have met people who are without doubt legally insane and yet appear on the witness stand to be rational. I must, in this case, be most careful not to allow Miss Harrison's obvious wit and intelligence to blind me to the fact that she could be suffering from a depressive illness … and so we all have to face the disturbing fact of the conflicting evidence … and remember that, however much one may sympathize with Miss Harrison in her cogently argued plea to be allowed to die, the law instructs me to ignore it if it is the product of a disturbed or clinically depressed mind. There are two recent cases that provide precedents. In the case of Miss B, the judgement was that as she was of sound mind and she had the right to turn off the respirator which would immediately result in her death. However in the case of Diane Pretty, it was held even up to the European Court, there was no right to assist in a suicide, no matter how compelling the circumstances might appear to be. I have to ask, then, is allowing Claire Harrison to discharge herself tantamount to assisting a suicide? Miss Harrison is a brave woman who is in complete control of her mental faculties and I believe her to be capable of evaluating the consequences – which may be prolonged and distressing – of her decision. She has asked to be discharged which will eventually result in her death. I have decided that allowing her to remove herself from the hospital does not make the hospital an assistant in her suicide. I shall therefore make an order that she be … set free.

A pause. The JUDGE *walks over to* CLAIRE.

JUDGE (CONT'D): Well, you got your hanging judge!

CLAIRE: I think not, My Lady. Thank you. Thank you very much.

3 **witness stand:** where a witness stands in court 7 **conflicting**: *sich widersprechend* 9 **cogently**: strongly and clearly 13 **of sound mind**: able to think rationally 15 **Diane Pretty**: British woman with motor neurone disease refused the right to die by the European Court of Human Rights in 2002 16 **compelling**: *schwerwiegend* 18 **tantamount**: equal 21 **evaluate sth.**: have an opinion about sth. after thinking about it carefully **prolonged**: continuing for a long time

The JUDGE *nods and smiles.*

JUDGE: Goodbye.

CLAIRE: Goodbye.

The JUDGE *turns and goes. She meets* DR. EMERSON.

JUDGE: Ah, Dr. Emerson.

DR. EMERSON: Yes?

JUDGE: I'm afraid you'll have to release your patient …

DR. EMERSON: I see.

JUDGE: I'm sorry. I understand how you must feel.

DR. EMERSON: Thank you.

JUDGE: Goodbye.

DR. EMERSON: Goodbye.

CLAIRE (TO MISS HILL): You won. Thank you.

MISS HILL *nods her thanks but doesn't trust herself to reply. She leaves quickly.*

The JUDGE *walks down the corridor.* DR. EMERSON *stands a moment, then slowly goes back to* CLAIRE'S *room.*

DR. EMERSON: Where will you go?

CLAIRE: I'll get a room somewhere.

DR. EMERSON: There's no need.

CLAIRE: Don't let's …

DR. EMERSON: We'll stop treatment, remove the catheter. Stop feeding you, if you like. If you refuse water, you'll drift into unconsciousness and die in a few days.

23–24 **drift into unconsciousness**: *in die Bewusstlosigkeit abdriften*

CLAIRE: You promise me there'll be no last minute resuscitation.

DR. EMERSON: Only with your express permission.

CLAIRE: Thank you.

DR. EMERSON *starts to exit.*

CLAIRE (CONT'D): Why are you doing it?

DR. EMERSON: Simple! You might change your mind.

CLAIRE: I won't. But thank you. It would obviously be easier for me if I stayed.

DR. EMERSON *nods and makes to go.*

CLAIRE (CONT'D): … Oh Doctor. Thank you for everything. It wasn't your fault. You have a good heart.

DR. EMERSON: … Known for it …

CLAIRE: … All over the world.

DR. EMERSON *smiles sadly and goes out.*

DR. SCOTT *stands and moves to the door. He turns and moves to* CLAIRE, *as if to kiss her.*

CLAIRE (CONT'D): Oh, don't. Better not, I think.

DR. SCOTT *smiles weakly and goes out. Lights hold on* CLAIRE, *as alone as anyone can ever be.*

BLACKOUT

2 **express**: clearly stated

ADDITIONAL TEXTS

Whose Life Is It Anyway? – Review by Peter Brown

Here in the UK, there's considerable discussion about the 'nanny state' – the extent to which the Government should interfere in the life of the citizen. Smacking children, banning smoking in public places, and the right of the individual to decide the manner and timing of their demise, are all hotly-debated items on the current political agenda. And almost every day brings new issues to the law courts to determine the rights and responsibilities of parents, spouses, doctors or patients in harrowing and complex 'life and death' cases.

It's not surprising then that Brian Clark's play 'Whose Life Is It Anyway?' has been revived – its subject-matter being as relevant today as it was when it won the Society of West End Theatre's best play award back in 1978.

The storyline is deceptively simple. Intelligent and vivacious sculptor, Claire Harrison, is recovering in hospital after a serious road accident has left her paralysed from the neck down. As the play opens, she has realised that the quality of life she can expect in the future will be so poor that she wishes to die. This decision leads to immediate conflict between Claire and her consulting physician, who sees his duty as preserving life, not terminating it. In the end, Claire has to resort to legal sanction in order to get what she wants.

'Whose Life Is It Anyway?' was first cast with a male (Tom Conti) in the role. When Conti left the production during its Broadway run, the lead was changed to a female one with Mary Tyler Moore in the role. Both Conti and Mary Tyler Moore won awards for their performances, but it does seem to work better with a female lead,

1 **nanny**: person who looks after children 5 **demise**: death **hotly-debated**: controversial 8 **harrowing**: shocking or frightening 11 **revive sth.**: give sth. new life 14 **deceptively**: in a way that makes you belive sth. that is not true 21 **sanction**: official permission 23 **run**: (of a play) series of performances

perhaps because it strengthens the conflict between the vulnerable principal character and the male-dominated medical team.

Better known for her role as Samantha Jones in 'Sex And The City' on TV (where she also spent a considerable amount of time in a horizontal position), Kim Cattrall makes her British theatre debut as Claire Harrison. It's an extremely demanding role because her movements are so severely restricted. However, Cattrall convincingly amalgamates the comedic aspects of the role with the desperation and isolation of her situation. And she's well supported by an able cast who have the challenging and delicate task of defining medical and legal professionalism without appearing totally inhuman. Ann Mitchell proves an authoritarian ward sister with a caring heart, and William Chubb strikes just the right tone as the paternalistic consultant.

My only quibble with the playing lies with Jotham Annan's performance as John (the ward orderly). Although he provided some necessary humorous relief, his actions were overstated – a case, I think, where a little less could have been more. However, he does introduce an extremely important dimension to the play when he raises the morality of the considerable resources spent on medical care in the west, compared with the paltry amount available to the developing world. It shows the kind of depth this play contains.

Lucy Hall's set design – using walkways on different levels and curtain tracks to segment the stage – cleverly suggests a busy modern hospital without littering it with the clutter of medical paraphernalia, enabling the audience to focus on the central character for much of the action, whilst fading her into the background when required.

Live theatre is certainly the best vehicle for serious issues of this kind. The intimacy and proximity of the cast challenges and provokes the audience in a way TV or film would struggle to do. However, I'm not as certain as Sir Peter Hall (director) that this play can be categorised so neatly as comedy because there's much in the

1 **vulnerable**: *verletzbar* 6 **severely**: *stark* 11 **authoritarian**: (here) strict
14 **quibble with sth.**: criticism of sth. 20 **paltry**: tiny 23 **segment**: divide
24 **litter**: (here) cover with unnecessary objects

play which is tragic, but the comedy is certainly required to make the piece work, which it most certainly does.

'Whose Life Is It Anyway?' is thought-provoking and unsettling on many different levels, but is definitely worth braving the winter cold to see, and to argue about afterwards.

Source: londontheatre.co.uk, 25 Jan 2005

3 **unsettling**: making you feel nervous or worried

Whose Life Is It Anyway? – Review by Michael Billington

What irony! Kim Cattrall, who deploys every inch of her body as *Sex And The City*'s Samantha, is forced to act from the neck up as the paralysed heroine of Brian Clark's revamped 1978 play. But, although Cattrall gives a tremendous performance, I feel the piece itself is much less open-minded than Clark and his director, Peter Hall, claim.

Clark's theme is the freedom to live or die; and he focuses the debate on a sculptor, Claire Harrison, who has spent five months in hospital with a severed spinal cord. Claire wishes to be discharged so that she can die: her consultant argues that it is his duty to keep her alive. Invoking the Mental Health Act, he also claims that her decision stems from clinical depression. Her solicitor counters with contradictory psychiatric evidence and refers Claire's case to law.

Clearly Clark advocates individual freedom. But how much freedom does he allow the spectator? Although the consultant is sympathetically played, Claire still has all the best lines.

Clark also loads the dice by presenting an upbeat social worker as an insensitive Miss Cheeryble. And it strikes me as a sin of omission that the religious argument goes unheard.

I admire Clark for dramatising a momentous issue. And by making the protagonist a woman rather than a man, as in the original, he turns the play into an intriguing battle against a medical patriarchy. But the debate has moved on since 1978.

And by invoking the examples of Christopher Reeve and Stephen Hawking on one hand and Diane Pretty on the other, Clark only reminds us that the moral issues are anything but clear-cut.

Still, Cattrall is superb as Claire: behind the surface resilience and smiling irony, she suggests a woman who demands the dignity of choice and aches with the loss of her sensual life. It is a major performance by someone who is infinitely more than a TV star; and

1 **deploy**: (here) use 3 **revamp**: improve 4 **tremendous**: very good 11 **invoke sth.**: (here) use sth. as a rule 12 **stem from sth.**: come from sth. 18 **omission**: thing that has not been included 20 **momentous**: very important 24 **invoke**: (here) mention 26 **clear-cut**: easy to identify 27 **resilience**: ability to survive

there is strong support from William Chubb as the dogged consultant, Ann Mitchell as a poker-backed Sister, and Janet Suzman as a humane judge.

Peter Hall's production, with its rushing sidelong movement, also avoids the cliches of a medical soap. But, in the end, the play is less a moral debate than a clarion call for Claire.

Source: The Guardian, 26 Jan 2005

1 **dogged**: determined, stubborn 2 **poker-backed**: strict and old-fashioned
6 **clarion call**: clear message

Dr. Albert-Reiner Glaap's Interview with Brian Clark

ARG: What caused you to – partially – rewrite "Whose Life" in 2005? Were you commissioned to do so?

BC: A West End producer Sonia Friedman of the Ambassadors theatre Group got in touch with me saying she thought it was time there was a revival of Whose Life. I talked with her and told her of the history of the play and that we had replaced Tom Conti on Broadway in the eighties with Mary Tyler Moore when he had to leave the production. She was intrigued with this idea and suggested we do the same in London. She asked who I would like to direct it and I said Sir Peter Hall, with whom I had worked in the National Theatre on *The Petition*. She liked that idea too. So Peter was approached, was interested and suggested Kim Cattrall as an actor who might be interested. She was.
As to the text we used, things had moved on. The central issue was unaffected by the passage of time, it is still illegal in the UK to in any way assist in a suicide. But there had been some events in the it intervening years which made the point even more urgent. Also, nursing practices, uniforms, relationships in hospitals and so on had subtly changed. It was a new production and I wanted it to be as up to date as possible. So I decided that it should be rewritten.

ARG: It seems to me that you have made four major changes/ alterations in the new version:
– the medical advances (possible generation of stem cells)
– the legal precedents (contrasting verdicts in the cases of Miss B. and Diane Pretty etc.)
– making Dr Emerson a more worthy opponent to the patient
– a woman in the leading role (as in the earlier version with Mary Tyler Moore)
Could you briefly comment on this? Is there anything important missing (i.e. other innovations)?

8 **intrigued**: very interested 14 **as to**: concerning 17 **intervening years**: years in between 25 **precedent**: *Präzedenzfall* 31 **innovations**: (here) new things

BC: Of course there were medical advances too – though none so great as to remove the central problem my character faces. And these had to be noticed in the new version.

There were too some new legal developments – though again none that rendered the play now irrelevant. I recall that a critic of the play (I think it was Michael Billington of The Guardian) noted at the time of the original production that here was a play that would still be playing in a hundred years. I thought that was daft! Surely in much less time than that a more sensitive law would be in place. But he was right and I was wrong. Whether or not the present state of the law will last for another sixty years is an open question but I am amazed it has not been changed already. I am sad that the play is still relevant.

The most important changes in the play are to the character of Dr. Emerson. There is a rule in Theatre that whoever is funny is right. This is certainly the tradition in English theatre. One thinks of the fools in *King Lear*, and *Twelfth Night* or the comic repartee in Restoration Comedy, where it is the wits who are right and the "straight" characters are pompous and indeed ridiculous. It is also a basic tenet of Drama that the core of it is conflict. I had come to feel very strongly – and indeed quite early in the life of the play – that the weakest part of the play was the characterisation of Emerson. He was not a worthy opponent for the protagonist. He was stuffy and humourless. This seriously weakened the play in my estimation. The protagonist won his exchanges with Emerson too easily. There was a lack of conflict. I started to remedy this in the screenplay of the film of Whose Life. We had a wonderful acerbic actor who played Emerson – John Cassavetes – and I rewrote Emerson to take advantage of the strength he was able to bring to the character. I continued this process in the new stage version, giving him (I hope) much greater wit and intellectual strength. It has also made him more dignified. I am now much happier with the characterisation of Emerson.

5 **render**: (here) make 9 **daft**: nonsense 17 **repartee**: funny comments and replies 19 **pompous**: arrogant 20 **tenet**: principle or belief 24 **stuffy**: boring 28 **acerbic**: critical and cruel

ARG: Do you consider the new text a necessary updated version? What is your reaction to some critics who claim that the play belongs to the time (the 1970s) in which it was written (which I disagree with!)?

BC: I think I have answered that question above. The law is the same – virtually.

ARG: Having seen the new version in London, I found that the 'comedy' of the play is much stronger than in the earlier versions (cf. the 'breast' scene, for instance). Was it your intention to make the play work even more on the intertwining levels of comedy and serious issues?

BC: Again, I have partly answered that above. It is important to understand in the tradition of English theatre there is no separation between comedy and seriousness. I recall a German playwright saying to me that he envied English playwrights because we could be comic and serious at the same time, whereas if he wanted to be taken seriously in Germany he had to be deadly serious. Yet my plays have been successful in Germany – perhaps we are regarded as the licensed fools of Europe – rather as the fools in Medieval courts. Perhaps because Shakespeare has given us permission! But actually the tradition predates him. In the medieval religious pageant plays, comedy and seriousness are inextricable. In the "Noah's Flood" play for example, Mrs. Noah is a comic character who nags Noah and refuses to get on the ark because she is talking with her "gossips." And in a Nativity play, there is a stage direction for Herod when he learns that Jesus has escaped to Egypt: "Here Herod rages on the pageant and in the street also." And we can imagine him running up and down the street raging away and causing great hilarity. It may be there is a real national difference. An Englishman, when he is in really serious trouble, often makes a joke about it. One of the wittiest

6 **virtually**: (here) almost 19 **licensed fool**: person who is allowed to be foolish 21 **predate sth.**: come from an earlier time than sth. 22 **pageant play**: play performed at a festival 23 **inextricable**: unable to be separated 29 **hilarity**: amusement

Englishmen in the last couple of hundred years was Winston Churchill. Many of the things he said, playwrights would have given their eye teeth to have thought of. There are dozens of examples of his wit – even at very desperate moments in the war.

With regard to the breast scene there is an amusing story about that. When I did the original change from a male to a female protagonist, the investors in the Broadway show were very concerned. Over and again they asked, "But how will you do the breast scene?" For the final run through we invited them to the rehearsal room. When we got to the scene, the tension rose. The male line was a straight piece of male flirting. "You have wonderful breasts." The woman's line "Do you like my breasts?" was so much more poignant. She goes on to tease the young doctor, "I am not about to jump out of bed and rape you or anything." And the mixture of comedy and sadness – revealing the desolation of the protagonist – is one of the most moving scenes in the play. After the run through one of the hard bitten investors said to me. "Tell me Brian, if you change this to have a man in the bed, how will you do the breast scene?"

ARG: I think the play is an improvement because Emerson's role has been strengthened, and, with that, also the conflict. And as the protagonist is a woman, the play is now also a battle against medical patriarchy. How would you argue for/against this?

BC: I think that the battle against medical patriarchy is there in the original version but it is stronger by changing the gender of the protagonist.

ARG: Why is there still no reference to Claire's parents or friends or...?

2–3 **give your eye teeth to do sth.**: want to do sth. very much 9 **run through**: rehearsal 15 **desolation**: extreme loneliness 17 **hard bitten**: tough (cf. p. 64)

BC: Not quite true. There is this for example.

> **DR. EMERSON**: *.... What about your parents? Are they living?*
>
> **CLAIRE**: *In New York. I thought it would break my mother – I always thought of my father as very tough. Typical working class. But it was the other way around. My father can think only with his hands. He used to stand around here, completely at a loss. My mother would sit there – just understanding. They were here a week ago – I got rid of my father for a while and told my mother what I was going to do. She looked at me for a minute. There were tears in her eyes. She said. "... it's your life ... don't worry about your dad – I'll get him over it." ... She stood up and I said, "What about you?" "What about me?" she said, "You're your own woman. I'm proud of you. Always was. Always will be ... ."*
> (TEARS ARE VERY CLOSE)
> *... I'd like to think I am my mother's daughter.*

There is also a reference to her fiancé somewhere or other. But on the whole I think the experience of the play is one of claustrophobia. It is the central metaphor of the play. And this is reinforced by having her life constrained by the hospital.

ARG: "Whose Life," needless to say, has an open ending. Whatever decision is to be made is left to the audience. The play is about individual freedom. Have you talked to spectators about the decisions they would make?

BC: Yes, frequently. Most say they would make the same decision. Whether they would in fact or not is an open question. I like to think I would make the same decision; whether I would or not is again an open question. But people do make the same decision as Claire. There are many examples.

19 **reinforce**: make stronger

Mental Health Act

The Mental Health Act was established in the United Kingdom in 1983 and applies to England and Wales. It was amended in 1987, 1995, and then significantly in 2007. It outlines the approach that should be taken regarding people with mental disorders, from their reception into the system, to their care and treatment.

Admissions can last from 72 hours to 6 months, depending on their reasons and whether the person is being admitted for assessment or for treatment.

The Act sets the rules regarding detention, assessment and treatment of patients against their wishes. For example, the Act says that if a mentally ill person refuses treatment for an unrelated physical illness, their wishes must be respected. However, if it is decided that the person does not have the mental capacity to give consent, or the physical illness is a direct result of their mental disorder, treatment can be given in their best interests. This ultimately gives doctors and other health professionals the power to decide how the patient should be treated, without the patient's consent.

THE AUTHOR

© Brian Clark

Brian Clark was born in 1932 in Bristol. He attended the Central School of Speech and Drama in London and then studied at the University of Nottingham. He taught in schools for eight years and was a staff tutor at the University of Hull from 1968–1972.

In 1970, he sold his play *Whose Life Is It Anyway?* to a production company and it was broadcast as a television program in 1972. He later adapted the teleplay for the stage. The reworked version premiered at the Mermaid Theatre in London's West End and starred the actor Tom Conti as Ken Harrison, the patient. The play won the 1978 Society of West End Theaters Award. Later that year, he brought the play to the United States.

In 1980, *Whose Life Is It Anyway?* was revived on Broadway, this time starring actress Mary Tyler Moore as the patient.

In 2005, Clark updated the play to better suit a female lead and to take into account more current developments in the debate on euthanasia and assisted suicide. It was put on in the Harold Pinter Theatre and starred the actress Kim Catrall (of *Sex and the City* fame).

Clark has written over 20 television screenplays including *Easy Go, Operation Magic Carpet, The Saturday Party, Achilles Heel* and *Telford's Change. Can You Hear Me at the Back* is his seond full-length stage play. More recent plays are *The Petitioner* and *Hoping for Byzantium*. His other theatrical works include *Post Mortem* and *Campion's Interview*.